From Billiard Balls to Bishops

To San and Mike

with best wishes

Ken   10/7/23

From Billiard Balls to Bishops

A Scientist's Introduction
to Christian Worship

Kenneth Alan Miles

RESOURCE *Publications* · Eugene, Oregon

Resource Publications
An Imprint of Wipf and Stock Publishers
199 W. 8th Ave., Suite 3
Eugene, OR 97401

www.wipfandstock.com

PAPERBACK ISBN: 978-1-6667-5924-2
HARDCOVER ISBN: 978-1-6667-5925-9
EBOOK ISBN: 978-1-6667-5926-6

03/23/23

To my Godchildren

Contents

Preface

"Why do you want to be a doctor?"

Emily had been expecting this question. She had rehearsed her answer after attending a course on how to prepare for medical school interviews.

"I have an interest in science and I enjoy helping people."

The interviewer was late middle-aged with a greying beard and glasses, just how you might expect a professor to look. "Why not become a nurse, then?" he asked.

Emily wasn't quite as prepared for this question.

"Well, I want to be able to diagnose as well as treat people," she replied.

"In that case, why not become a physiotherapist? They diagnose and treat patients."

Emily was beginning to feel uncomfortable. In truth, she couldn't quite put into words the reasons why she wanted to be a doctor. It was simply something she felt she was called to do. It was her vocation.

Interviews often went like this when I had the privilege of sitting on appointment panels for medical school. I'm not sure I could have voiced my reasons for wanting to study medicine when I was seventeen years old. Even now, more than forty years later, I find it hard to pinpoint the particular skills a doctor needs. But I have discovered that one key attribute is an ability to weigh up information from multiple different sources to create a short list of possible diagnoses and develop a plan of investigation and treatment for the patient. A doctor has to integrate scientific knowledge about the human body and human disease with the patient's symptoms, the findings on clinical examination, and the results of various investigations such as blood tests and X-rays. Treatment needs to be chosen with a view to the patient's personal preferences and their social circumstances. In many healthcare systems, the cost implications of the investigations and treatments must also be factored in.

In much the same way, when I became a Christian in my second year of medical school, it was only natural to try to integrate this new (to me) way of looking at things with the science and medicine I was learning at the time. On occasions, the task has proved challenging, and it remains a work in progress to this day, but the journey has been made that much easier by reading the works of many great authors who have explored the interface between science and faith: John Polkinghorne, Nancey Murphy, John Lennox, and Alister McGrath, to name but a few. I never found the issue of evolution by natural selection particularly problematic. But for many years, the question of how God interacts with the physical world was a stumbling block for me.

"The idea of engaging with science is often being approached more as an argument to be won or with the sense of engaging with a tiger in a cage. It may be a brave thing to do but we'll leave it to the experts and they'll do it."[1] This is how the Archbishop of Canterbury, Justin Welby, described the attitude of some within the church when he introduced a conversation on science and faith ahead of the 2022 Lambeth Conference for Anglican bishops. Most people experience faith as a personal encounter with God, and a reluctance to engage with science may reflect a concern that the disengagement and objectification required for scientific analysis precludes a personal encounter. Yet, every day, doctors and other healthcare professionals have to undertake scientific analysis *during* a personal encounter with a patient. This would not be possible if personal encounters were precluded by science.

On the other side of the equation, some people from a scientific background fear that belief in God may be equivalent to committing "intellectual suicide." They have an expectation that faith requires a completely different style of thought from the scientific approach which, as John Polkinghorne has pointed out, seeks to develop and evaluate an evidence base of experiences before attempting to formulate wider forms of understanding. Presentation of religious knowledge as "handed down from God," and hence unquestionable, will therefore be particularly problematic for scientifically minded individuals.

Yet the relationship between science and religion need not, and arguably should not, be portrayed in this way. It is entirely possible to

1. Lambeth Conference Conversations, "Talking About Faith and Science."

uphold science and Christianity at the same time. For me personally, science has enriched my commitment to God. It is important to recognize that the way scientists exclude supernatural causes in the study of the natural world is a research strategy rather than a belief about the nature of reality. This realization allows scientific data to be reinterpreted without assuming the non-existence of causes beyond nature, leading to a deeper understanding of the natural world.

Science has been a fascination for me since childhood, when I was particularly captivated by astronomy. Later I switched from mapping the stars to mapping the human body as my medical career took me into the fields of diagnostic radiology and nuclear medicine. Most chapters in this book include a medical case history, usually one that involves the use of X-rays or other types of medical imaging. These stories are either fictional or publicly available in the medical literature. Where I have based them on real clinical situations, for reasons of confidentiality the details and the patients' names have been changed.

The science that underpins the use of X-ray and other forms of radiation for medical diagnosis includes physics and biology, which are both important crossing-points between science and faith. My academic work has also given me a grounding in the scientific evaluation of evidence. These experiences have inevitably shaped my quest to integrate science and faith, hopefully providing a different slant from other writers in this field. This book reflects where I am on that journey today.

Why write about the science of worship? At a time when church attendance is falling, there is a need for new ways to attract people to services of worship. For many people, church services can seem inaccessible or even a bit weird, and a clearer explanation of what happens in church could encourage more people to attend. Not knowing why things are said and done in particular ways can make people reluctant to take up an invitation to attend church. It can also lead people of faith to give up public worship and choose to practice their faith by other means, and is a reason that many individuals give for not attending church. A fresh explanation of worship that blends science and Christian thinking may be particularly compelling, considering the high regard given to science in Western societies.

Some faith communities have responded to falling attendance by developing new styles of worship, sometimes called fresh expressions of church. Although a good idea, these initiatives are not always developed on the basis of evidence of effectiveness. A book that pulls together scientific data about the effects of individual acts of worship could help to identify forms of church service that are more likely to be successful.

Lastly, among the many books written about the interface between science and faith, some have contended that a closer integration of these disciplines can lead to a deeper level of understanding. A combined scientific and religious account of public worship would provide a real-world demonstration of that principle.

My writing unavoidably focuses on Christian worship, not because I consider all other religions to be untrue, but simply because it is the tradition I grew up in and is therefore most familiar to me. The concept of God that emerges as the book progresses reflects this background. First, God is viewed as a reality that is more than the natural world of space–time, matter, and energy. Next, the natural world is portrayed as being created by God and in every moment dependent upon God for its existence. Finally, God is a reality that interacts with the natural world that is dependent upon it. Although grounded in Christianity, this picture of God is sufficiently broad that much of what is written could apply to other faiths.

This book has been written with two kinds of reader in mind. First, it is for anyone who currently does not go to church. Research has shown that people who seldom or never go to church are more likely to say that science and religion are in conflict, and for some this misunderstanding may be a barrier to attending public worship. Others may be reluctant to go to church simply because they find it hard to make sense of the worship process. If either of these concerns apply to you, it is my hope that the arguments for taking experiences of God seriously and the scientific accounts of what happens in church will make you think again.

For those who already attend church, this book will hopefully offer a deeper understanding of worship. The contents may also be helpful to people of faith who find an apparent conflict between science and religion to be a cause for doubt. Research has shown that there are many who are in this avoidable position. The book is not intended to be a work of apologetics that aims to convince people of the truth of Christianity. That goal would be beyond the scope of this book, not least because I have focused on scientific data rather than historical events. Historical evidence is fundamental to Christianity, particularly the facts around the life, death, and Resurrection of Jesus of Nazareth. But as a scientist venturing into the realms of theology, I already feel exposed and even less qualified to consider the evaluation of historical information in any detail. Nevertheless, the book does present some new arguments which may be of interest to anyone studying apologetics.

The title, *From Billiard Balls to Bishops*, is taken from chapter 10 which uses billiard balls to explain chaos theory and its potential interactions with quantum uncertainty. By way of illustration, I include a chaos-based model for church attendance which shows sensitivity to initial conditions (sometimes called the "butterfly effect"). The attendance of one additional member of the congregation at week 0 is found to significantly reduce attendance at week 10 – not a good outcome if that happens to be the week when the bishop is due to visit. I have since discovered that the game of billiards features within an iconoclastic TV miniseries called *The Young Pope*. On one occasion, the character Cardinal Voiello is depicted playing billiards with a small, fluffy, white dog sitting on the table. The connection to my title would have been even closer if, rather than a dog, it had been Schrodinger's cat!

I could not have completed this book without the help of others. In particular, I would like to thank my wife, Anne. Without her encouragement and support, this project would never have been completed. I am also indebted to Adrian, Keith, Claire, Roderick, Sally, and Ian, who gave up their time to read and comment on early drafts. Their input has been invaluable. I would also like to thank Nicki for her excellent copy-editing.

Introduction

Informed Worship

WE ALL STAND UP. The organ plays a slow melody, and we join in singing. A small procession starts to move from the front of the church down the central aisle, into the middle of the congregation. The aromatic smoke from burning incense fills the air. We turn slowly to face the procession as it passes. The cross mounted on a long staff and the tall candles held up by those leading the procession transit across the backdrop of the church columns stretching upwards to the roof. Carried high in the center of the procession is the Gospel book which will soon be read aloud by the priest.

"If he's going to read from the Bible, why doesn't he just stand at the front and do it?" thinks Hannah, a science student who has come to church for the first time at the invitation of her friend Mark. The more skeptical of Hannah's fellow students had told her she would have to leave her brain at the door if she was going to church. They had reminded her what Astrophysicist Carl Sagan had said, that science is "informed worship." But they were mistaken. If Hannah had brought her understanding of human biology to church, she might have begun to recognize how this seemingly arcane ritual could affect the minds and bodies of the churchgoers. A deeper understanding of public worship would require additional knowledge that as yet was unfamiliar to her. She would need to combine her science with Christian thinking.

Religious services are rich and full of beauty for some, yet to others they can often seem strange and obscure. But churches are not museums for the preservation of ancient rituals. The words and actions performed during worship are the way members of a faith community express their conviction that we are all invited into a fuller, freer life through a renewed relationship with God.

There are many ways to explain what happens during worship, but one comes from an unlikely source: science; not pure science but science blended with Christian thinking. Scientific knowledge can be looked at afresh while allowing for the existence of God. This may not be such an odd idea. The natural world which science tells us about is important to Christians. The Bible describes how the natural world takes part in worship (e.g., Psalm 148; Revelation 4), and items from the natural world play a central role in some forms of worship: water in Baptism, bread and wine in the Eucharist. The natural world also includes our physical bodies.

If science and religion are in conflict, as is commonly portrayed by the media, then the idea that science could be part of an understanding of Christian worship may come as a surprise. But perhaps it is less surprising if we recall that modern science emerged in a Christian context and that many of its basic assumptions have their origins in Christian thinking. The idea that the natural world is rational and open to human understanding reflects the rationality of its divine creator, and the expectation that there should be laws governing nature arises from a belief in a divine lawgiver. The ability of humans to understand the rationality of nature follows from the belief that mankind was made in the image of the God who created the world.

A close merger between scientific and religious thinking is essential if we are to develop a science-based guide to worship. Without this integration, the application of science to public worship will bring with it a way of thinking that denies the supernatural, reducing the human person to a largely unconscious, unreliable, and selfish product of brain physiology. But science need not be seen as a threat to faith, and this book does not aim to explain away religious practice. Rather, scientific knowledge can enrich the Christian thinking behind worship practices. To blend science and faith in this way, we need to recognize that science simplifies reality by excluding the supernatural in order to better understand the natural world. In the same way, the London Underground map is a simplified representation of reality with the specific purpose of guiding passengers around the transport system. The Underground map poses no threat to an understanding of life above ground. Although not strictly science, reinterpreting scientific observations in a context of faith offers a fuller understanding of God as revealed through his creation.

Worshipping in church is one way in which people respond to experiences of God. Worship therefore takes for granted that there are experiences in which God is truly and critically a part. Experiences of God can affect people in different ways. For some, they will lead to a decision to commit to a life of faith. Others may say such experiences do not provide enough evidence to persuade them of God's existence. Many try to explain them away altogether.

Every experience that we consider to be an encounter with God is ultimately an event within our brain. And our brains can be mistaken. Perhaps we have misinterpreted a sensation of some kind and suffered an illusion. Those who hold to a worldview that excludes the supernatural will always come to such a conclusion. Others may be more open to the possibility of genuine encounters with God but have never had a convincing encounter themselves and consider that the subjective experiences of others are insufficient reason to act on the possibility. In other words, the worldview and beliefs we bring to any experience will determine the interpretation we put upon it. It is therefore pointless appealing to experiences of God as a motivation for worship unless we have resolved, as best we can, these philosophical questions.[1]

But are religious experiences a good basis for worship? Part 1 of this book argues that experiences of God are sufficiently common to be worthy of inclusion in serious theorizing. Rather than discounting such experiences and so risking the loss of unique insights about the cosmos and human life, they can be evaluated by applying the scientific principles behind a method known as evidence-based medicine, which is how doctors make decisions for patients even when the available science is less than perfect. Despite inevitable uncertainties, the evidence for the reality of religious experience is shown to be a rational motivation for participation in worship.

The congregation at a church service is not an audience watching a performance. Saying or singing words that express Christian thinking is clearly important. But Christian worship is not just about what is said. The congregation also takes part in worship by adopting certain postures and movements, such as kneeling and bowing their heads. These worship actions are often performed in unison, which requires the worshippers to watch each other and to be observed themselves, so that the movements are aligned. But the bodily postures and actions performed during worship

---

1. C. S. Lewis makes the same point when considering miracles: Lewis, *Miracles*, 11–13.

are not arbitrary customs adopted only for their symbolic meaning. Worship actions also affect the way our bodies work, altering physiological processes such as blood pressure, heart rate, and breathing. In turn, these changes influence our emotions, thoughts, and decision-making. It is only fitting that knowledge of how the human body works should help an understanding of these aspects of worship.

Part 2 will look at the ways in which the biological responses brought about by worship actions can bring about a range of beneficial outcomes and suggests that a scientific understanding of worship can be seen as a Christian act of offering creation back to God.

By and large, worship is informed by the Bible and Christian thinking. I am neither a trained biblical scholar nor a theologian and shall not consider these aspects for worship in any detail. Those who assume that experiences of God do not happen or are an inadequate basis for worship are unlikely to be swayed by Scripture or religious doctrine. My undertaking is to present a different but complementary perspective on worship as a way of engaging readers who may later wish to look further into the more biblical explanations of the purpose and meaning of worship.

Carl Sagan was widely recognized as a great science communicator. Although he did not consider himself an atheist, his views on science and religion were strongly endorsed by the New Atheist movement. The flip side to Sagan's view that science is informed worship is that we should regard religious worship as uninformed. But it seems he did not consider the possibility that, when combined with Christian thinking, science itself can help to inform religious worship. At a time when church attendance is falling, and given the way communicators such as Sagan have sparked a broad enthusiasm for science, a science-based account of what happens during worship might encourage more people to join in.

—— Part One ——

Experiencing God

1

The Spherical Cow

SYLVIA WAS A SIXTY-FIVE-YEAR-OLD woman who collapsed during coffee-time at her church after the morning service. A doctor in the congregation came to assist and found Sylvia semiconscious but unable to move her right arm. She was also slurring her speech. Paramedics were called and Sylvia was taken to hospital, where she was rapidly transferred to the Radiology department for a computed tomography (CT) scan of her brain. This diagnostic test involves rotating an X-ray tube around the patient to generate images representing slices through the brain. An injection of contrast material, or "dye," was then given into a vein in Sylvia's arm so that additional images depicting the blood flow to her brain could be produced. These images showed an area of reduced blood flow caused by a blood clot in the artery to the left side of Sylvia's brain (i.e., a stroke). With this information, doctors were able to give Sylvia an injection that dissolved the clot. Over the next few days, Sylvia regained the use of her arm and her speech improved.

Radiologists use CT scanners to portray all parts of the body, from head to toe, from the smallest bone in the middle ear to the liver, the largest internal organ in the body. Artificial intelligence computer programs are now used to help the radiologist interpret the images more confidently, and hybrid devices combining CT with radioisotope imaging have been developed so that abnormal areas that accumulate the radioactivity can be pinpointed more precisely.

The science of decision analysis makes sure that these devices are used in ways that bring about the best health outcomes at reasonable cost. As imaging techniques have become more complex, the amount of data about the human body provided by an imaging test has increased enormously. Some examinations can comprise more bits of information than is contained in the human genome! In the field of cancer, image features are being matched to specific abnormalities in the DNA of a tumor so that doctors can select the best treatment for each patient. These studies have shown that DNA does not completely determine the tumor's destiny. There is not always a one-to-one relationship between a particular abnormality in the tumor DNA and the biological behavior of the tumor shown by scans. The imaging information therefore complements the results from analysis of the tumor's genetic material. More and more, medical imaging is showing things inside the body that would otherwise remain hidden, short of resorting to the surgeon's knife.

The technique that demonstrated the blood flow to Sylvia's brain was first performed by a group of researchers I led at Cambridge, UK. We used a mathematical model known as the Fick principle to calculate the blood flow from the way the amount of contrast material Sylvia had received changed in her brain and blood over time. When developing this method, we made the assumption that the brain is an "instantly mixed compartment." This assumption simplified the model so that it was workable. The use of simplifying assumptions like this one represents an important part of scientific methodology and provides an effective way to deal with complexity. It allows scientists to arrive rapidly at a solution to a problem without being sidetracked by all of its details. Complex objects might be simplified to spheres, air resistance avoided by envisaging the object in a vacuum, motion may be assumed to be frictionless, and surfaces infinitely large. Everyone realizes these assumptions do not match reality, but they allow scientists to tease out the fundamental principles that underlie the way the natural world works.

Simplified representations of reality are used not only in science, but also in everyday life, and they can be very helpful provided they are used in the setting for which they were designed. A good example is the well-known map of the London Underground transport system mentioned in the introduction. The map has been drawn up with two assumptions: a) the direction between one station and the next is either vertical, horizontal, or at 45 degrees, and, b) the precise distance between any two stations is irrelevant. The map works well if you are travelling on the Underground system but would be very misleading if you were to try to use it to find your way around London above ground.

Within science, the use of simplifying assumptions is so widespread that it has become the subject of a famous joke about a dairy farmer who is hoping to increase milk production. The farmer seeks the help of a theoretical physicist at the local university. After carefully studying the problem, the physicist tells the farmer, "I have a solution, but it only works if we assume a spherical cow in a vacuum." The joke helps us to remember that simplifying assumptions are not necessarily true, and this was the case for our blood-flow method. An instantly mixed compartment does not exist, and the assumption clearly does not match reality.

When presenting our method to other scientists, I was once asked why I had not allowed for mixing of X-ray dye within the brain. Had I been quick enough, perhaps I could have borrowed the answer that the renowned French mathematician and astronomer, Pierre- Simon Laplace (1749–1827), gave when presenting his work on the stability of the solar system to Napoleon. The Emperor is said to have asked why God did not appear in his calculations. Laplace's now famous reply was, "I have no need for that hypothesis." But if I had answered in this way, the assumption of instantaneous mixing would still not be true. Rather, the technique merely works without the concept of mixing, as shown by Sylvia's story.

The "Only Natural Causes" Assumption

When scientists employ simplifying assumptions, they should be explicit about their use, acknowledging that these assumptions may not necessarily represent reality. Ideally, at some point there should be an assessment of how much the solution is affected by the underlying assumptions. For our blood-flow method, the findings of later studies that allowed for mixing of the X-ray dye within the brain were very similar to previous work. The model was therefore insensitive to the assumption of instantaneous mixing. Similarly, the concordance between Laplace's model of the solar system and observed data was unaffected by whether God existed or not. So, rather than say, "I have no need of that hypothesis," Laplace could have said that his model was insensitive to the question of God's existence. In his book, *God is not Great*, atheist journalist Christopher Hitchens even acknowledges that Laplace could have responded along these lines,[1] but Hitchens fails to recognize that, by being more honest about the underlying simplifying assumptions, such an answer would have been more scientific.

1. Hitchens, *God Is Not Great*, 66–67.

Nonetheless, Laplace has been adopted as something of a champion by atheists today. His encounter with Napoleon is cited to support the view that matter is the fundamental substance in nature, and that all phenomena, including mental phenomena and consciousness, result from material interactions. "In any of its forms, the God Hypothesis is unnecessary," says Richard Dawkins in *The God Delusion*.[2] And yes, the absence of the supernatural is an assumption that underpins all of science. But as we have seen, scientific assumptions are not necessarily true. Science merely operates *as though* there is nothing outside nature. Science, therefore, does not in itself preclude the possibility of God.

Questioning Assumptions

Sylvia experienced difficulty in speaking during her stroke because a blood clot had prevented blood reaching a part of the brain involved in the production of speech. This brain region is named after the French physician Pierre Paul Broca (1824–1880), who first recognized its importance for language. Broca was a highly productive researcher who is also known for the following quote: "The least questioned assumptions are often the most questionable." The notion that only natural properties and causes exist is possibly the least questioned assumption in science and, for the most part, scientific explanations are entirely unaffected by the issue of whether there is anything beyond nature. But the assumption may become questionable when science investigates areas that are inherently sensitive to assumptions about the supernatural, such as studies of spiritual experience or evidence for the existence of God. To retain the "no supernatural causes" assumption in these circumstances would be like trying to use the simplified map of the London Underground as a way to navigate the more complex reality above ground.

A proper assessment of our brain blood-flow method required a re-examination of the data without using the simplifying assumption of instantaneous mixing. But when discussing religious faith, many skeptics seem to forget the basic scientific principle of acknowledging simplifying assumptions. Rarely do they seem to question the assumption that only natural properties and causes exist. Some may go even further by saying that it is an intolerable presumption on human reason to question this assumption. They speak as though it is religious people who need to

2. Dawkins, *God Delusion*, 68.

show that the simplifying assumption they use is false, when it should be the other way around. Since this opinion is frequently affirmed in books by eminent scientists and philosophers, and instilled into the minds of children at school, it is unsurprising that a willingness to consider the possibility of a reality beyond nature is regarded by some to be a mark of an uneducated mind or even mental illness.

But what if the same circumstances were to apply to the spherical cow? In the joke, cows were simplified to spheres as a way to solve a particular problem, and we can say the same thing about the assumption that only natural explanations are real. But suppose schools were to teach children that simplifying a cow to a sphere was an accurate representation of reality, and this concept were reinforced in books by well-known scientists and academics, all backed up by the scientific principle which says simple theories are more likely to be correct. If this were so, the belief that a cow is more complex than a sphere might also be thought of as ignorant or crazy.

Scientific data and evidence evaluations related to belief in God should be re-evaluated without assuming the non-existence of causes beyond nature. It can even be argued that there is an ethical responsibility to do so in order to avoid any negative consequences that might otherwise result from inappropriately implementing the "Only Natural Causes" assumption. The assumption need fail just once for the onus of proof to fall on those who assert it to be an accurate representation of reality rather than a simplifying assumption. In fact, there are various situations in which this assumption breaks down, including those outlined in this book. Although some may wish there were no God, there are good reasons to question this dogma of scientific atheism.

Whose Science Is It Anyway?

It is not necessary to believe in God to enjoy a sense of awe from studying the natural world. But we are now so familiar with the idea that the universe exhibits a law-like character, it is easy to forget that this concept is founded in Christian thinking. If we had started with a belief in a blind and pitiless universe with no purpose, as described by New Atheist Richard Dawkins, it might have been difficult to find the inspiration to study the natural world at all. A worldview that believes exclusively in natural properties and causes can only see the benefits of the scientific endeavor as an unlikely but fortunate coincidence. Yet, the countless studies of the natural world undertaken by early Christians show us how science fits comfortably within a Christian context where its success is not seen as owing to chance but as a gift from God.

In their book *Let There Be Science*, David Hutchings and Tom McLeish give many examples of where Christianity has proved to be an inspiration to the progress of science. The oldest book in the Bible, Job, can be seen as an invitation to the conduct of science through the broad array of questions about the workings of the natural world that are posed within its pivotal nature poem (Job 38:16–30). The book of Daniel describes what seems to be the first ever recorded controlled trial (Daniel 1:12–15), a research method that is widely used in medicine today (see also chapter 5). There have also been several people of faith who have demonstrated an approach to the study of the natural world that presaged the science we now consider modern. These include Robert Grosseteste, the Bishop of Lincoln from 1235 to 1253, who advocated controlled experiments and anticipated not only the big bang theory of the origin of the universe but also wave-particle duality of quantum physics. In addition, the English Benedictine monk the Venerable Bede (672–735) observed that fresh water floats above salt water because it is lighter, and so undermined the belief of his time which thought the sea remained salty despite being fed by fresh river water because fresh water sinks.

Is Scientific Knowledge a Barrier to Worship?

Several notable atheists have suggested that intelligence and scientific knowledge cause people to reject God. They cite research showing an inverse correlation between intelligence and religiosity,[3] or low rates of belief in God among scientists. In his book, *The God Argument*, atheist philosopher A. C. Grayling goes as far as suggesting that ignorance of science is contributing to "the continuance of religious belief in a world which might otherwise have long moved beyond it."[4] With this statement, Grayling makes it clear that he believes scientific knowledge causes a rejection of faith. But are such conclusions supported by evidence?

It is easy for the unskilled to misinterpret a correlation between two factors. Typically, an association is confused with a causal relationship in

---

3. Interestingly, the reported trends are less marked when religiosity is expressed as church attendance rather than religious belief.

4. Grayling, *God Argument*, 13.

which one factor is assumed to bring about a change in the other. However, this need not be the case. There could be a third variable underlying the change in both of the factors studied, or the association may simply have occurred through chance alone. Consider, for example, the association between paramedics and road traffic collisions. Paramedics are highly likely to be found at road collisions, and the bigger the incident, the greater the number of paramedics. Although there is a clear correlation between the number of paramedics and the size of road traffic incident, no one would suggest that paramedics *cause* traffic collisions.

Measures of correlation are used in science to evaluate how strongly two factors are associated, for example the number of cigarettes someone has smoked and their risk of developing lung cancer. But additional criteria were needed to establish that smoking causes cancer. In 1965, the English epidemiologist and statistician Sir Austin Bradford Hill (1897–1991) outlined several aspects of an association between two factors that should be considered before concluding the presence of a causal relationship.[5] Scientists have adopted these criteria ever since.

We can apply the Bradford Hill criteria to determine whether there is any evidence to support the claim that scientific knowledge causes people to reject God. Let us consider one particular study discussed at length in the *The God Delusion* by atheist Richard Dawkins. In 1997, Edward Larson and Larry Witham reported the results of a survey which found that the majority of US scientists either disbelieved or expressed doubt in the existence of God, a rate that was significantly lower than that found in the general US population.[6] Richard Dawkins offered this data as evidence that "there might be something wrong with religion."[7]

When applying Bradford Hill's methodology, the first criterion to consider is the strength of the association. The stronger the association between a risk factor and outcome, the more likely the relationship is to be causal. However, almost 40 percent of the scientists surveyed believed in a God who "is in intellectual and affective communication with humankind."[8] The association can therefore only be considered weak.

Next to consider is the consistency of findings. Have the same findings been observed among different populations, in different study

---

5. Hill, "Environment and Disease."

6. Larson and Witham, "Scientists Are Still Keeping the Faith."

7. Dawkins, *God Delusion*, 128.

8. Larson and Witham, "Scientists Are Still Keeping the Faith."

designs, and at different times? A recent study of US professors found the rates for belief in God to be highly variable in different groups of scientists, being highest among physical scientists and lowest for psychologists and sociologists.[9] The relationship between scientific knowledge and disbelief is therefore inconsistent.

The specificity of the association should also be evaluated. There should be a one-to-one relationship between cause and outcome. However, similar surveys of levels of belief among other professions indicate that disbelief is not specific to scientists. For example, a survey by James Leuba in 1935 demonstrated that the rates of disbelief in God expressed by scientists were similar to those found among dramatists and playwrights.[10]

The temporal sequence of the association is important. Exposure to the causative factor should precede outcome. If scientific knowledge leads to disbelief, it should not be possible for scientists to become Christians. However, there are well-known cases where this has happened, for example Francis Collins, head of the US National Institutes of Health and leader of the human genome project, and the astrophysicist Hugh Ross. I would also consider myself to be among them.

Dose-response effects represent another criterion. Changes in the outcome should follow from corresponding changes in exposure. The amount of science taught in schools has increased significantly over time. Yet when Larson and Witham compared their results to an earlier study from 1918, they found no significant change in rates of disbelief among scientists, implying the absence of a dose-response relationship.[11]

The most robust criterion is experiment: Does the removal of the exposure alter the frequency of the outcome? Clearly, in this case, this test cannot be applied as it is impossible to remove scientific knowledge once gained.

The established criteria for providing evidence of a causal relationship therefore *do not* support the idea that scientific knowledge causes people to reject belief in God. This conclusion is perhaps unsurprising given that science emerged in a Christian context. But it is surprising that some notable atheists should conclude otherwise. Despite their stated commitment to the scientific method, these skeptics seem to confuse association and cause through uncritical and superficial analyses of research data.

9. Gross and Simmons, "Religiosity."
10. Brown, "Conflict."
11. Larson and Witham, "Scientists Are Still Keeping the Faith."

Has research shown an alternative cause for why people of faith are underrepresented in scientific disciplines? Data for Christians in the USA has identified two potential factors: stereotypes portraying Christians as being less competent,[12] and a perception that scientists are biased against Christians.[13] Both factors would tend to lead people who believe in God to select other careers. There is some anecdotal evidence for similar stereotypes in the theatre professions, another line of work that is identified with disbelief in God.

Combining Science and Christian Thinking

The most tiresome and uncreative question that can be asked about science is whether it is the only valid means for obtaining truth about the world and reality. The question is trivial because to answer "Yes" is self-contradictory—scientific enquiry cannot demonstrate that science is the only way to truth. But there is also the unresolved issue of how to define what counts as science. For example, alchemy—the transmutation of elements—is not considered scientific. Yet every day, all around the world, imaging of patients with cancer is undertaken using the radioisotope fluorine-18 which has been transmuted from oxygen-18 in a particle accelerator known as a cyclotron. Despite these obvious internal inconsistencies, an excessive belief in the power of science to establish truth has prevented many from questioning the underlying assumption that nothing exists beyond nature, and this is despite the fact that questioning assumptions is fundamental to the scientific method.

One of the greatest advances in science was the discovery of X-rays in 1895. The latter half of the nineteenth century was a time when Darwin's theory of natural selection had seeded the notion of a conflict between science and religion. But if such a confrontation was underway, it did not deter the Reverend George H. Ide of Milwaukee, Wisconsin, from combining Christian thinking with the science of X-rays in a sermon he gave in July 1896. He saw the discovery of X-rays as pointing to the existence of a spiritual world and envisaged a kind of X-ray in the world of spirit that allowed God to see into the human soul: "Christ knew what was in man. He used the X-rays to discern the thoughts and intents of the heart. He sees through us, for we are transparent. It may be we entertained the

---

12. Rios et al., "Negative Stereotypes."

13. Barnes et al., "Are Scientists Biased?"

delusion that our thoughts were known only to ourselves. But the X-rays of His vision disclose them."[14]

Reverend Ide was not the only person to connect X-rays and religion. The first ever X-ray image of a human had been taken just eight months before his sermon, in the days leading up to Christmas 1895. It showed the hand of Anna Bertha Roentgen, complete with wedding ring. She had not suffered any injury, nor did she have any pain in her hand. She was simply helping her husband, Wilhelm Roentgen, who had discovered a new kind of ray a few weeks before. But Anna was horrified by the sight of the bones of her hand, exposed but alive, and is said to have cried out, "I have seen my death." She refused to set foot in her husband's laboratory ever again.[15]

Although the public rapidly embraced Roentgen's discovery, initially many people reacted in the same way as Bertha. The way X-rays seemed to dissolve skin and muscle to leave just the skeleton was reminiscent of the bodily decay that occurs after death. X-rays were invisible yet cut through things—like light, only deeper, revealing parts of themselves that until then had been visible only to God. One contemporary writer referred to "fearful powers" in play.[16]

Rather than something disturbing, people are now more inclined to see X-rays and scans as fundamental to the healing that can be obtained through modern medicine. This transition is the result of several decades of applying the sciences of physics, biology, and decision analysis to turn the disquiet about X-rays into understanding. Even now, just like the Reverend Ide's sermon, combining these sciences with Christian thinking can offer new ways to enhance religious faith. The great impact of X-rays and other medical imaging techniques comes from their ability to provide evidence. Imaging can reveal the presence and nature of disease or injury and show whether things are getting better or worse. They reduce diagnostic uncertainty and influence decision-making, and the extents to which medical imaging can produce these results are used as objective markers of their effectiveness. Just as the science of medical imaging can reduce diagnostic uncertainty and support decisions about treatment, the same principles have the potential to reduce uncertainty about God and support decisions concerning a life of faith.

14. Ide, "X-Rays."
15. Lentle and Aldrich, "Radiological Sciences."
16. Gunderman and Tritle, "First-Generation Radiography."

An important advance in medical imaging science over recent decades has been the development of devices that combine two types of imaging technique in a single examination. For example, Computed Tomography, as used to diagnosis Sylva's stroke, can be combined with Positron Emission Tomography, a technique that will feature in later chapters. The use of these hybrid technologies has become widespread because they provide a deeper understanding of disease, showing not only how the structure of tissues is affected, but also the organ's function.

Combining faith and science can work together in a similar way. As soon as we discard the "No God" assumption, we can no longer consider the line of enquiry to be science. Nevertheless, this strategy does represent a justifiable extension of the scientific method that offers a deeper understanding of the natural world and God's relationship to it, something that theologian scientist Alister McGrath has called "a theology of nature."[17]

As well as providing deeper insights, combining science with theology creates opportunities for using scientific methods to interrogate atheist claims about belief in God. We have already used this approach in this chapter to successfully challenge the assertion that scientific knowledge causes people to reject God. Several more examples of this approach are found elsewhere in this book.

Christian author C. S. Lewis wrote, "In science we have been reading only the notes of a poem; in Christianity we find the poem itself."[18] Like poetry, the network of experiences and theories that make up Christian thinking is complex. Science cannot prove the existence of God, but science is accustomed to dealing with complexity and, similar to the notes of a poem, it can help us interpret the meaning of experiences of God. In turn, this richer understanding of spiritual experience can translate to a deeper appreciation of faith and a greater commitment to public worship. Rather than undermine belief in God, it is possible to use science for faith.

---

17. McGrath, *Enriching Our Vision*, 169.

18. Lewis, *Miracles*, 158.

2

Shattering the Celestial Teapot

IMAGINE THAT YOU HAVE woken up with pain in your stomach. It's been hurting for a few days, but today things have got much worse. You decide to go to the hospital where you are seen by a doctor (let's call him Dr Richardson). He examines you and arranges for a CT scan of your abdomen.

A little while later, Dr Richardson tells you that the radiologist has told him the scan shows acute appendicitis. So you ask Dr Richardson what he is going to do for you, and you are taken aback when he says, "Unfortunately, there is nothing I can do."

Shocked, you ask what will happen to you.

He says you might get better on your own, but probably you will get sicker and die.

"You must do something," you plead, but he replies, "There has never been a randomized controlled trial comparing surgical removal of the appendix to no treatment. Until those trials are done, there is not enough evidence to say that surgery is going to help."

You say, "But my uncle had appendicitis and he got better after his appendix was removed."

"I am not going to base treatment decisions on anecdotes like that. I only base my medical decisions on hard evidence," he says, and calls for the nurse.

Of course, doctors do not behave like Dr Richardson. They frequently make decisions based on less-than-perfect evidence. The surest way to know that a medical treatment works is to do a randomized controlled trial in which patients are randomly selected to receive either treatment or a sham treatment known as a placebo. Yet studies in different clinical environments have shown that treatment decisions are made without randomized controlled trial evidence in approximately half of cases.

Are doctors being unscientific when they use lower-level evidence? The answer is no. In fact, they are applying science to the assessment of evidence. If randomized controlled trial data is available, doctors should base their decisions on those studies. When high-level evidence is not available, it is important to assess the quality of the data obtained from less-rigorous forms of research. All low-level evidence is not considered equal. For example, non-randomized trials with several patients would be given more weight than a single case report.

There are a number of reasons why high-level evidence may not be available for any given circumstance. In many situations, randomized controlled trials would be unethical because it would be necessary for some patients to receive no treatment or a treatment thought to be less effective. For rare diseases, it may be impossible to recruit enough patients into a trial to obtain this high-level evidence. The scientific evaluation of evidence may even go as far as determining whether it would be worthwhile doing the trials that would give better evidence. This approach, known as the Expected Value of Information method, is discussed further in chapter 8. It compares the benefits of having the highest level of evidence to the costs of obtaining that evidence. If the benefits do not outweigh the costs, it may be acceptable to make treatment decisions using currently available lower-level information.

Faith and Evidence

Many skeptics criticize religious faith on grounds of lack of evidence. For example, Richard Dawkins is quoted as saying, "Faith is belief in spite of, even perhaps because of, the lack of evidence."[1] But when making these criticisms, atheists have rarely, if ever, been clear about their approach to the evaluation of evidence for the existence of God. Reading between the lines, it seems there is an unstated assumption that evidence should be limited to data that can be obtained at will (i.e., is repeatable), at least in principle. All lower levels of evidence are simply rejected out of hand without considering why such evidence might not be available for religious experience and offering no criteria for evaluating lower levels of evidence. In short, they seem to have forgotten the science of evidence

1. Dawkins, Speech at the Edinburgh International Science Festival.

synthesis. This oversight is comparable to the disastrous misjudgment made by the fictitious doctor who would not remove your inflamed appendix in the story we considered earlier.

Yet, many experiences may not be obtainable at will, not just encounters with God. Philosopher Phillip Wiebe has highlighted how excluding such experiences from any consideration could mean that potentially unique insights about the cosmos and human life are overlooked.[2] We therefore need a method to grade lower levels of evidence based on this sort of data. It is possible to base this method on three criteria for assigning weight to evidence from experiences that are not obtainable at will.

1. Is the experience widespread?

Citing Stephen Braude, Wiebe has proposed a category of experiences that cannot be obtained at will, but are sufficiently common to be worthy of inclusion in serious theorizing. This "semi-experimental" evidence should be given greater weight than anecdotal experiences (often one-offs) that are insufficiently numerous to be thought believable. This approach is directly analogous to that used by doctors in medical decision-making.

Wiebe uses the example of near-death experiences to show how an experience, although not obtainable at will (for good reason), can be reported widely enough to be considered in serious theorizing. In a near-death experience, a person who was very close to death has memories of a deeply spiritual experience such as meeting dead friends and family members or seeing a white light during the time when death was near. Wiebe points to how early scientific reports of near-death experiences were initially met with skepticism, despite (or perhaps because of) their similarity to the visionary journeys that have been described since antiquity. But as reports of similar experiences accumulated in large numbers from around the globe, skeptics began to accept that these experiences really do occur.[3] A similar approach can be adopted for experiences of God.

The weight of evidence is increased when a widespread set of experiences has features that are constant over time and across cultures. This is because the experiences are more likely to have been gained independently rather than by the influence of one person upon another. For near-death experiences, a core set of elements such as bright lights and encountering

2. Wiebe, "Religious Experience," 513.
3. Wiebe, "Religious Experience," 503–22.

deceased persons can be found in accounts both from antiquity and from different parts of the world. The identification of these core elements has contributed to the recognition of near-death experiences as worthy of inclusion in serious theorizing. Experiences of God similarly show core features that are consistent over time and across cultures.

But what if those undergoing the experience are poorly informed or unenlightened? Should we still give evidential weight to their experiences? Some people have raised this concern about those who experience God. Whether people of faith are in fact unenlightened is highly debatable. Regardless, as Princeton University philosopher Thomas Kelly points out, "the cumulative opinion of a large number of people often provides significant evidence even when it conflicts with the opinion held by a comparatively smaller group of people who are in a better position to judge."[4] This principle can be illustrated by considering the use of diagnostic tests in medicine. No diagnostic test is 100 percent accurate. There are cases where the test results are positive even though the disease is absent, as well as cases where the results are negative when the disease is present. Consider a situation where three tests are available for diagnosing a particular condition. One is more accurate than the other two in that it is less likely to return a positive result when the disease is absent. The probability of a false positive result with this test is only 2 percent. The other two tests are much more likely to return a false positive result, with probabilities of 8 percent and 10 percent respectively. The first test can be considered "better informed," and the lower false positive rate can be likened to a lower likelihood of wrongly concluding that a given experience was an encounter with God. If you apply only one test, the first is clearly more accurate. But if you apply the two less-accurate tests, the chance that both are falsely positive is 8 percent multiplied by 10 percent, which equals 0.8 percent, less than the 2 percent chance from the more-accurate test alone. By analogy, an assembly of less-informed opinions that agree can be more accurate than a smaller assembly of opinions that are better informed. As noted by French surgeon and past winner of the Nobel Prize in Physiology or Medicine, Alexis Carrel, "A few observations and much reasoning leads to error; many observations and a little reasoning to truth."[5]

Often, those expressing the opinion that people who experience God tend to be less well informed already believe that nothing exists beyond the

4. Kelly, "*Consensus Gentium*."
5. Carrel, "Famous Maxims."

natural world of matter and energy. This standpoint goes hand in hand with the notion that human cognition is purely the product of evolution. But evolution is a chance process that is orientated towards survival rather than truth. People holding this view therefore need to consider whether their cognitive faculties can be relied upon to draw accurate conclusions about evidence for and against the existence of God (see chapter 7).

Another potential objection relates to whether religious experiences, although widespread, are too varied to be considered as evidence for one phenomenon. This is often expressed as, "There are so many gods, they can't all be true." Even as far back as the sixteenth century, the French theologian and reformer John Calvin (1509–1564) recognized that God may choose to reveal himself in ways that are appropriate to the circumstances and level of understanding of those undergoing the experience. If God tailors his revelation to the individual in this way, there will inevitably be variations in experiences of God across cultures and over time.

Furthermore, humans are biological entities and, as such, it would be unrealistic to expect responses to God to be completely consistent across cultures and over time. Variable responses to a common cause are well recognized in medicine. Every medical student learns that a single disease may produce very different signs and symptoms in different patients. And there is a medical adage which says that "uncommon presentations of common diseases are more common than common presentations of uncommon diseases." In the same way, the variability of religious experience is more likely to reflect different encounters with one God rather than distinct encounters with several different gods.

2. Is the Experience Part of a Network of Interconnected Experiences and Theories?

Using semi-experimental data as evidence is constrained by the problem of circularity. How can you know that an experience has the hallmarks of an interaction with God without first knowing something about what God is like? As philosopher Nancey Murphy points out, similar problems of circularity also happen in science.[6] Consider this experiment, for example. You have a closed container of gas that is being heated by a Bunsen burner. Attached to the container, there is a constant volume gas thermometer and a pressure gauge. You record the pressure and temperature

6. Murphy, "What Has Theology to Learn?"

as the container heats up. When you plot the paired temperature and pressure measurements on a graph, you get a straight line, confirming the combined gas law: the pressure of a gas multiplied by its volume is equal to a constant times its temperature.

But notice that you are using the gas thermometer to provide evidence for the gas laws, even though you cannot know that the thermometer is providing reliable measurements unless you know the gas laws. The reason why this situation does not undermine the experiment is because there is an interconnected network of theories and other experiments which, as a whole, makes the evidence from a gas thermometer reliable. The same principle can be applied to semi-experimental data: it will be more reliable as evidence when part of a network of interconnected experiences and theories.

3. Does the Experience Change Behavior?

A further limitation associated with semi-experimental data is the problem of subjectivity. Religious experiences are typically private and not open to public examination or replication by others. There is also the possibility of self-deception. Murphy suggests that we can address this issue by looking for the impact of the experience on behavior, because these effects can be witnessed by others.[7] It is always possible that certain changes in behavior, such as a demonstrable increase in gladness, could simply result from self-deception. But other changes in behavior are less likely to be because of self-deception, including actions that are costly to the individual concerned and changes that persist over an extended period of time. Example of such actions include significant acts of charity and ongoing attendance at public worship. Self-deception is also less likely to be a factor if the members of the community in which they live exhibit similar changes in behavior.

Shattering the Celestial Teapot

A rigorous scientific assessment of evidence for God's existence would therefore develop criteria, such as those above, to enable a systematic evaluation of data that, for good reason, cannot be obtained at will. To insist that

---

7. Murphy, "What Has Theology to Learn?"

only the highest levels of evidence can be valid is a form of lazy thinking which, if applied in medicine, would be potentially disastrous.

Had the New Atheists adopted a thorough scientific approach to evidence, they might have thought twice about mentioning Russell's celestial teapot. The celestial teapot is an analogy that Philosopher Bertrand Russell (1872–1970) specifically applied to belief in God. He wrote:

> If I were to suggest that between the Earth and Mars there is a china teapot revolving about the sun in an elliptical orbit, nobody would be able to disprove my assertion provided I were careful to add that the teapot is too small to be revealed even by our most powerful telescopes. But if I were to go on to say that, since my assertion cannot be disproved, it is intolerable presumption on the part of human reason to doubt it, I should rightly be thought to be talking nonsense. If, however, the existence of such a teapot were affirmed in ancient books, taught as the sacred truth every Sunday, and instilled into the minds of children at school, hesitation to believe in its existence would become a mark of eccentricity and entitle the doubter to the attentions of the psychiatrist in an enlightened age or of the Inquisitor in an earlier time.[8]

Russell's teapot has subsequently influenced more explicitly religion-parodying concepts such as the Invisible Pink Unicorn and the Flying Spaghetti Monster. But the celestial teapot and its copies are poor analogies for God. First, unlike the celestial teapot, God is not proposed as an additional entity within natural world. Rather, the entire natural world is in every moment dependent upon God for its existence. What's more, the analogy has an overly simplistic view about how to evaluate evidence.

If we compare Russell's teapot to belief in God using the scientific approach to evidence described above, it is immediately obvious that the claim that God exists should be given considerably more weight than the existence of the celestial teapot. The fact that experiences of God are widespread and have been reported since antiquity and across all cultures justifies the inclusion of God's existence in serious theorizing. This is hardly the case for Russell's teapot. There is also no network of experiences and theories around the existence of the celestial teapot, whereas experiences of God form part of a network of experiences and theories that make up the system of thought known as theology. Furthermore, it is hard to envisage what costly behavior might demonstrate belief in the celestial teapot—drinking

8. Russell, "Is There a God?"

excessive amounts of tea, perhaps. On the other hand, people who claim to experience God commonly take up lifelong behaviors that are costly to themselves, such as acts of charity and regular attendance at worship, actions that often spread among the communities in which they live.

The celestial teapot fails as an analogy for belief in God. But Bertrand Russell was not a scientist, and the current scientific methods for evaluation of evidence were developed after his professional life. It is perhaps understandable that he did not use the systematic approach to evidence outlined above. The same cannot be said for professional scientists or other scientifically inclined individuals who continue to quote Russell's teapot and similar religious parodies today. Is it not time these individuals actually approached the evidence for God more seriously?

Evidence and Ethics

There is a possibility that the objection held by Dawkins and others against the use of evidence from experience is not a scientific one, but one based on ethical concerns. They might simply think that it is wrong for anyone to base their beliefs on evidence that is not repeatable. Although holding a belief without repeatable evidence is not harmful in itself, actions arising from that belief can be. Even if an individual ensures that this is not the case for them, permitting belief without evidence in general would give justification to other beliefs that can lead to harm.

In a previous conversation with British journalist Justin Brierley, Dawkins acknowledged that his value judgments are a product of his evolutionary past and are therefore random, as is any product of evolution.[9] If Dawkins thinks that people ought not to base their beliefs on evidence that is not repeatable and objective, then he presumably considers this assertion to be a random product of evolution as well. Ideas of right and wrong are merely biological processes defined, for instance, by the patterns of brain activity that have been demonstrated by scanning the brains of volunteers while they ponder ethical questions.

How should we respond when someone who believes only in natural properties and causes expresses an ethical concern about use of evidence? If the feeling that I ought not do something is simply a biological process, then we could respond in the same way as we might when someone describes any other biological sensation, such as a feeling of nausea. If

9. Brierley, *Unbelievable?*, 132–33.

someone says, "I feel sick," it would be nonsensical to say, "Yes, I see that you are right." But we might say, "I am sorry to hear that." So, if the sense of right and wrong really is simply a matter of biology, perhaps sympathy would be the appropriate response when Dawkins says we ought not uphold a belief without objective evidence. His assertion would hardly be a reason to change our view.

For anyone holding to a faith that is committed to love of one's neighbor, the idea that the way we believe could inadvertently cause harm demands serious attention. We should not believe carelessly. Indeed, Christians are charged with always being "prepared to make a defense to any one who calls you to account for the hope that is in you" (1 Peter 3:15). A responsible approach to belief requires us to consider not only the harms that might follow from lowering standards of evidence, but also the potential benefits that could be lost if we were to disallow beliefs that cannot be supported by high-level evidence. The story at the beginning of the chapter illustrates this clearly. It would be highly unethical to not remove an inflamed appendix merely because of a lack of a randomized controlled trial. Similarly, the benefits arising from belief in God, such as giving to charity and working for peace and justice, would be lost if religious faith were to be rejected owing to lack of data that is obtainable at will. Belief in God should therefore be worthy of serious consideration based on the semi-experimental evidence described above.

3

First Do No Harm

JOHN IS ONE OF the many selfless people who volunteer to be a subject in a medical research study. Without people like John, it would not be possible to base medical diagnosis and treatment on evidence. Medicine would not have advanced from the days when individual healthcare professionals would have to make their decisions based on the opinions of well-known doctors (sometimes called eminence-based medicine) and their own judgment and experience—a time when quack treatments were commonplace.

John is taking part in a study that aims to determine the right dose of a new drug for treating cancer. Laboratory experiments have shown that the drug attacks abnormal blood vessels within a tumor. The project uses the same CT technique as that mentioned in chapter 1 to diagnose Sylvia's stroke, but this time the scans will measure the blood flow in a tumor in John's liver. John will have two scans: one before receiving the new drug and another during the treatment. The change in tumor blood flow will be compared with the dose of the drug he receives. By repeating this technique in different patients at different drug doses, it will be possible to find out the dose that has the maximum effect on blood flow without causing serious side effects.

Early in the development of a new drug, it is important to run studies like this to show that the drug can be used safely. This approach follows the principle of "first do no harm," which forms part of the code of medical ethics known as the Hippocratic Oath. (Although this principle is contained within the Hippocratic writings, the first use of this exact phrase is not found until the seventeenth century.) In evidence-based medicine, demonstration of safety comes before demonstration of effectiveness. It is equally important to show that belief in God is not harmful before expressing that belief in acts of public worship.

Many skeptics assert that religion is harmful. There has been a resurgence in these claims following the recent emergence of terrorism that appears to be inspired by religion. Similar assertions have been made in the past, based on other examples of religiously associated violence such as the Crusades, the Hundred Years' War, and the troubles in Northern Island. But the claims of harm go beyond the violence that is associated with an apparent commitment to God. For example, merely bringing up a child as Christian has been likened to child abuse.

These criticisms of religious faith make two assumptions: a) there is an agreed standard of harm against which the effects of religion can be judged, and b) an association between religious identity and violence indicates that a commitment to God causes harmful behavior. As we have seen in chapter 1, identifying and justifying assumptions is an essential part of the scientific process. Despite their apparent high regard for science, skeptics rarely seem to acknowledge or test these assumptions. So let us examine them here.

We also need to define what is meant by "religion." I understand religion to be a set of practices and behaviors that bind people together in a common quest for knowledge and/or experience of God. Public worship is one expression of this quest. This definition sees religion as relating to a God who is an objective reality and specifically excludes quasi-religious practices based on a god of one's own making. It is all too easy to invent a god as a justification for violence, or any other unjust behavior. To quote the American novelist Anne Lamott, "You can safely assume you've created God in your own image when it turns out that God hates all the same people you do."[1]

Harm and Morality

How do we decide whether something is harmful? Cutting someone with a knife may be considered harmful, for example, but not if performed to remove a cancer. The American legal philosopher Joel Feinberg points out that our concepts of harm are closely linked to ideas of right and wrong.[2] We condemn those actions that not only reduce someone's well-being but also are wrongful. For instance, accepting a job promotion might reduce the

1. Lamott, *Bird by Bird*, 22.
2. Feinberg, *Moral Limits.*

well-being of a colleague who also applied for the same promotion, but would not be considered to be a harmful act because there was no wrongdoing.

There is good evidence to show that in all cultures, people recognize the difference between doing something bad and doing something good, but people decide whether an action is right or wrong in different ways. Some weigh up the good and bad effects of an action and assess its overall outcome. Actions that are likely to cause the greatest wrong overall or least overall good are the ones that are to be condemned. Others decide the rightness or wrongness of an action by whether it upholds or breaks certain moral principles that everyone is duty-bound to obey. Rather than being personal opinions or social conventions, these principles are seen as something we discover, similar to how we determine mathematical facts. Actions are denounced when they are inconsistent with these principles.

Many examples of moral dilemmas that aim to tease out these different approaches to moral decisions have been published. The following life-boat scenario is one example:

> You are on a cruise ship when there is a fire on board, and the ship has to be abandoned. The lifeboats are carrying many more people than they were designed to carry. The lifeboat you're in is sitting dangerously low in the water—a few inches lower and it will sink. The seas start to get rough, and the boat begins to fill with water. If nothing is done it will sink before the rescue boats arrive and everyone on board will die. However, there is an injured person who will not survive in any case. If you throw that person overboard the boat will stay afloat and the remaining passengers will be saved. Is it appropriate for you to throw this person overboard in order to save the lives of the remaining passengers?[3]

One person might answer "yes" to this because the injury caused to one person is outweighed by the benefit of saving the lives of many. Another individual might answer "no" because breaking the moral principle of "do not kill" is wrong, regardless of the consequences.

Azim Shariff and Jared Piazza are psychologists with a research interest in the relationship between religion and morality. Along with their research associate Stephanie Kramer, they have brought together evidence from several studies to show how religious and non-religious people tend to use different approaches when resolving questions of right and wrong.[4]

---

3. Greene et al., "Neural Bases."
4. Shariff et al., "Morality and the Religious Mind."

Imaging studies have also shown that each approach is associated with a different pattern of brain activity. When confronted with moral choices such as the example above, individuals who believe in God are more inclined to make decisions based on moral principles, while non-religious people tend to weigh up the positive and negative outcomes of an action. Religious subjects are also slower to make their decisions, which could reflect an attempt to resolve conflicts between the moral principles and the overall outcome.

Harm to Relationship with God

People of faith generally believe that human well-being is enhanced by being in a proper relationship with God. And there is evidence to support this claim. Regular attendance at public expressions of worship is associated with fewer health problems and a longer life span, not only in comparison to people who are socially isolated but also relative to those who are supported by secular social networks.[5] Contemplative practices such as focused prayer and meditation reduce stress which, if chronic, increases susceptibility to a wide range of illnesses. An attitude of mind inspired by experiences of God can also activate health-enhancing mind–body interactions.

Unlike non-believers, religious people may take into account any impact on their relationship with God when deciding on the moral significance of an action. It is possible that an action will be considered harmful because it is detrimental to this relationship, even though it might have no impact on well-being from a purely worldly perspective. These kinds of acts may also conflict with some of the practices and behaviors that bind together a religious community in their quest for God. The stance that some religious groups hold towards certain types of sexual conduct can be seen as an example of this broader understanding of morality.

An Agreed Standard of Harm?

Because harm and morality are closely linked, differences in the understanding of right and wrong between religious and non-religious people mean that there can be no agreed standard against which it is possible to judge whether

5. Kark et al., "Does Religious Observance Promote Health?"

religion is harmful. So on what basis do atheists assume that their definition of harm is correct? They might argue that definitions of harm solely based on damage to a relationship with God should be discounted because, in their view, there is insufficient evidence for God's existence (even though there is at least sufficient evidence to take the possibility seriously). But even without those considerations, significant differences in the approach to right and wrong remain. Furthermore, it is not possible to argue that a rule-based approach to morality is also dependent upon belief in God because studies have shown that non-religious subjects frequently adopt this approach for certain acts, such as killing and torture.

Often, those who assert that belief in God is harmful hold to a worldview that allows for only natural properties and causes. As highlighted in the previous chapter, from this perspective, the feeling that something is wrong is simply a biological process. "I feel this is wrong," becomes equivalent to, "I feel sick." If this is so, different approaches to matters of right and wrong must simply represent biological variability. One or other may confer greater evolutionary advantage, but this would not make it correct. Nature selects for reproductive success and survival, not truth.

Some may argue that responding to certain acts as though objective moral principles do exist is simply part of what it means to be human. It would be inhuman to do otherwise. But the use of technologies is also part of being human, a quality that has undoubtedly contributed to human survival. These technologies include tools that can modify human biology, such as drugs and behavioral therapies. If the moral sense is simply a product of human biology, then why not develop these technologies to modify our feelings of right and wrong? Maybe we could control our feelings of ought and ought not in the same way that we might take a drug to suppress nausea. But if this were possible, what principles would we use when deciding whether to take the drug? Perhaps we ought not use the drug if it were to harm the well-being of others. But notice another judgment about right and wrong has crept in, one that is also potentially controllable. Under the influence of the drug, there would be nothing to stop us from acting in ways that would benefit ourselves at the expense of others.

The idea of developing drugs to control our feelings of right and wrong may seem to fall within the realms of science fiction. This is unsurprising because most people feel and act as though their moral sense is more than mere biology, regardless of their intellectual position on the existence of things beyond nature. As outlined in the previous chapter, if a widespread experience and its impact on behavior are inconsistent with the associated network of theories and experiences, the evidence base for those theories is undermined. And this is the case when human morality is interpreted within a worldview in which only natural properties and causes are considered to exist. On the other hand, feeling and acting as though objective moral principles do exist is entirely compatible with a network of theories and experiences in which God is recognized as the source of moral intuition.

Cause or Association?

There is a joke about an alcoholic who wanted to reform. He had noticed that when he drank whisky and soda, he got drunk. The same was true when he had vodka and soda, and again for brandy and soda. So he decided to cut out the soda. This anecdote highlights the dangers of mistaking an association for a causal relationship. Although drinking soda was associated with being drunk, it was not the cause. And the same applies when considering whether religion causes people to perform harmful acts. This question is complicated further by the lack of a clear standard of harm, as discussed above. But we can address this difficulty by restricting our analysis to issues where people tend to adopt a similar rule-based approach to moral decision-making regardless of whether they are religious or not, namely killing and torture.

Few people would doubt that religious affiliation was associated with killing and the use of torture during the Spanish Inquisition of the Catholic Church in the fifteenth century. But we should not assume that these associations show that being committed to God *causes* people to perpetrate violence when in fact there are alternative explanations. On the face of it, a causal relationship seems unlikely, given that almost all religions hold to the Golden Rule: do to others what you would have them do to you (see, for example, Matthew 7:12).

Fortunately, there are well-established scientific methods for evaluating evidence for a causal relationship between two events found together. Developed in the 1960s by English epidemiologist and statistician Austin Bradford Hill, these methods are widely used in evidence-based medicine to avoid inappropriate withdrawal of beneficial medical procedures on account of invalid interpretations of study results.[6] In chapter 1, we used

6. Hill, "Environment and Disease."

these criteria to reject the idea that scientific knowledge causes people to reject belief in God, and we can use the same approach to assess the relationship between religion and violence.

To recap, when looking for a causal relationship, the first step is to consider *the strength of the association*. The stronger the association between a risk factor and outcome, the more likely the relationship is to be causal. In other words, the more violent people there are among religious communities, the more likely religion is the cause for the violence. Yet only a tiny minority of religious believers commit acts of terrorism or other forms of violence, and so the association can only be considered weak.

The *consistency of the findings* is also important. A causative relationship would be supported by finding the association repeatedly in different populations at different times. In her book, *Fields of Blood*, Karen Armstrong has undertaken a detailed study of the history of the relationship between religion and violence. From her work, it is clear that the expression of violence within religious communities has varied considerably between different faith traditions and within the same tradition over time.[7] Moreover, a research study of adolescents in the USA has found that religious attendance is associated with a decreased likelihood of violence.

The *specificity of the association* is the next feature to weigh up. If the effect is only infrequently found with other factors, the more likely the relationship is causal. But it is abundantly clear that there are many elements other than religion that have been associated with terrorism and violence. In fact, it has been estimated that more deaths have resulted from secular wars than from religious conflicts. Examples of secular terrorists include Joseph Stalin, who is widely quoted as saying, "The easiest way to gain control of the population is to carry out acts of terror," and the Tamil Tiger movement who developed the practice of suicide bombing before it was adopted by religiously inspired terrorists.

The *sequence in which the associated events occur* provides a further indication of the likelihood of cause: exposure to the cause must precede outcome. In other words, we need to ask whether people have been exposed to religion before or after becoming violent. Criminal psychologist Marc Sageman has profiled more than 500 jihadists, including those involved in the 9/11 terrorist attacks in the USA. He found that the majority

---

7. Armstrong, *Fields of Blood*.

had been brought up in secular homes and attended secular schools, and only adopted Islam after joining Al-Qaeda.[8]

Further evidence of a causal relationship may be provided by what are called *dose-response effects*. An increase in exposure to the supposed causative factor should be matched by an increase in the outcome. In other words, for religion to be the cause of violence, a greater exposure to religion would be associated a greater propensity for violence. In 2014, Mohammed Nahin Ahmed and Yusuf Zubair Sarwar were arrested on their return to Heathrow Airport after eight months fighting for Islamic State in Syria. At the subsequent trial it was revealed that, ahead of their trip, the two terrorists had ordered online *Islam for Dummies* and *The Koran for Dummies*. In his study, Marc Sageman found that such a superficial understanding of Islam was typical among his subjects, concluding that their fervor for violence "results from their *lack* of religious training, which prevents them from evaluating their new beliefs in context."[9] A greater exposure to religion seems to reduce the likelihood of committing acts of terror.

Perhaps the strongest evidence of a causative relationship is provided by studying *what happens when the supposed causative factor is removed*. Is there a matched change in the outcome? There have been a number of instances in history where religion has been forcibly removed from society. Perhaps the most notable are initial years following the French Revolution and the Soviet regime under Stalin. Neither period is renowned for a lack of violence. If anything, violence was worse.

Using a science-based approach to evaluate the evidence, it is not possible to conclude that a commitment to God causes violence. Recalling the joke about the reforming alcoholic, just as soda dilutes the effects of alcohol, it is equally possible, or even more likely, that a commitment to God weakens the human predisposition to violence.

Hijacking Religion

What alternative explanations could lie behind the fact that religion and violence are often found together? We can begin to understand this association by returning to the story of John who is receiving a drug that attacks abnormal blood vessels within his tumor. For centuries, it has been known that more blood vessels are found in and around cancers than in normal tissues.

8. Sageman, *Leaderless Jihad*, 47–70.
9. Sageman, *Leaderless Jihad*, 60, my italics.

It would be easy to conclude that too much blood is the cause for the disease, and this thought process may have lain behind the practice of bloodletting as a treatment for cancer. Today, we know this is not the case. Tumors need a supply of blood to provide the oxygen and nutrients that are required for their rapid growth. Chemical substances released by the cancer cause new blood vessels to grow into the tumor from normal blood vessels nearby. In effect, cancers hijack a blood supply from the surrounding healthy tissues. Under a microscope, the new tumor blood vessels are not like those seen in healthy tissues. Instead of the normal regular formations, tumor blood vessels are distorted and arranged erratically so that the blood is supplied unevenly. Today, patients can benefit from drugs that exploit these differences and block the formation of these new blood vessels.

In a similar way, religion can be hijacked by those looking to undertake violence. Just as a tumor needs a blood supply, in order to attract new members, terrorists and other violent organizations need justifications that support their cause, and they look to religious texts to find them. But just as tumor vessels are distorted and supply blood to the tumor unevenly, the interpretations of Scripture used to support violence are distorted and quoted out of context.

Is there evidence to support this model for religiously associated violence? Studies into religious behavior have shown that there are people who approach religion as a means to a non-religious end.[10] They use affiliation with a faith community to gain benefits such as security, support, prestige, or self-justification. Furthermore, research has demonstrated that people who approach religion in this way are reluctant to allow the existence of opinions or behaviors that differ from their own. In fact, greater levels of intolerance are seen in this group than among non-religious people. Intolerance can be expressed in a number of ways. It can lead to verbal and emotional mistreatment, and to the imposition of restrictions on certain individuals or groups. But intolerance can also be a trigger for violence.

Thankfully, religious people are rarely violent in the Western world today. The kinds of benefits sought by those who approach religion as a means to an end are typically much more moderate. Examples include opportunities to make friends or access to comfort in times of trouble or sorrow. But this reflects the current lack of social and political significance for religion in Western societies today. In previous times in the West, and in some cultures today, being part of a particular religious

10. Batson, "Individual Religion."

group also meant greater social standing and political power. And when this is the case, religion may be identified as a means to achieve more sinister non-religious objectives.

Karen Armstrong gives compelling arguments that in many cases political motivation is a more plausible factor driving violence associated with religion. Religion is simply hijacked for political gain. She also points out that many are inspired to join Islamic terrorist groups by a desire to respond to the suffering they see within Islamic communities in the Middle East, suffering which in good measure may be attributable to previous foreign policies of secular Western nations.[11] Political motivations can also be identified for the Crusades and the Spanish Inquisition.

Religion as End or Quest

People of faith do not represent a uniform group with an identical approach to religion. Some approaches to religion are linked to less intolerance and even increased compassion. Rather than seeing religion as a tool to achieve a non-religious aim, many people see religion as an end in itself. They sincerely believe the teachings of their religion and try to live their life by them. And there are people who see religion neither as a means to an end nor as an end in itself, but as a search for truth. Although having some features in common with those who see religion as an end, these individuals are more willing to tackle deep questions about the nature of reality without resorting to quick and easy answers. They accept doubt as part of what it means to be religious and are open to updating their beliefs to accommodate new information.

American social psychologist C. Daniel Batson has undertaken a wide-ranging review of how the different approaches to religion are related to intolerance and compassion.[12] Studies have shown that measures of intolerance for people who see religion as an end are almost always lower than those who see religion as a means, although only comparable to non-religious people. However, these results apply only to intolerances disallowed by their faith community. Levels of intolerance are increased when the intolerance is not specifically prohibited by their religious community. The lowest levels of intolerance are seen among those who see religion as a quest for truth, and this applies regardless of whether the intolerance is disallowed by their

11. Armstrong, *Fields of Blood.*
12. Batson, "Individual Religion."

community or not. In fact, such individuals show high levels of compassion and are willing to help others with different opinions and behaviors, provided the help they give does not promote intolerance.

How can a faith community be welcoming to all people while constraining the intolerance associated with seeing religion as a means to an end? This is a difficult but important question for faith communities. One way could be to encourage all members of the community to adopt the beliefs, attitudes, and behaviors that are associated with lower levels of intolerance. For example, teaching could encourage flexibility in religious thought. Complexity and uncertainty can be acknowledged as inevitable parts of a commitment to God while offering ways to deal with these challenges in a positive manner. Commitment to God can be portrayed as a journey in which ideas about God evolve over time, paralleling the progressive change in religious thought that is readily apparent in Scripture.

Environmental and social psychologist Benjamin Meagher has shown that people with different approaches to religion tend to be more or less comfortable with particular worship spaces.[13] People who see religion as a quest for truth generally report more positive experiences in worship spaces that are visually complex and open to exploration; settings in which the more you move around, the more there is to see. The opposite has been found for people who see religion as a means to an end. These findings open up possibilities for arranging worship spaces in a way that encourages the approaches to religion associated with greater tolerance and compassion.

Using Science for Non-scientific Ends

It seems some people (perhaps many) have an approach to science that mirrors the way certain individuals see religion as a means to an end; people who use science to achieve non-scientific goals. Science can be hijacked to support these aims in a similar way to religion. I have experienced this first-hand when science meets politics. And history has shown that using science in this way can lead to violence. Consider, for example, the scientific justification for the Nazi Holocaust.

Science is also used by some to attack religion, including the claim that belief in God is harmful. We have seen how those who misuse religion to support political violence typically have a superficial understanding of Scripture. In the same way, those who condemn religion as a source of

13. Meagher, "Deciphering the Religious Orientation."

violence seem to be unaware of, or have chosen to ignore, the science and evidence outlined in this chapter. Would it be unreasonable to expect them to have applied the scientific methods they hold so highly to their assessments of the relationship between religion and violence?

4

Unbelievable Electrons

Now in his early seventies, Andrew still enjoys walking to his local shops to buy a few things and maybe stop for a cup of coffee. But recently his right calf has started to hurt when he is walking. The pain eases off when he stops and rests, and he used to be able to get to the shops before things got too bad. Now he can only manage fifty meters or so. Last month, Andrew had a CT scan of his legs, and this showed the cause for his walking difficulty. He has a narrowing in the artery that supplies blood to his right leg. His doctor explained that without a good blood supply, his leg muscles will not get enough oxygen and start to hurt.

Today, Andrew has returned to the X-ray department for treatment. Dr Jones, the radiologist, is going to open up the narrowed artery with a tiny balloon. Before she starts, Dr Jones explain the procedure to Andrew. "First, I will clean the skin in your groin and cover you up with sterile drapes to keep everything clean. Then I will inject local anesthetic around the artery in your groin."

"I won't be asleep, then?" asks Andrew.

"No, there's no need for that. This is only a minor procedure."

Once the local anesthetic is working, I will pass a narrow tube called a catheter into the artery in your leg. Using the X-ray machine to guide me, I will position the catheter into the narrowed part of your artery. The catheter has a small balloon on it which I will inflate for a short while. And this should open up the artery so that you won't get the pain when you walk."

"Will I feel the balloon inflate?"

"No, you should feel nothing at all."

Andrew's treatment is known as percutaneous transluminal angio-plasty and was invented by an American radiologist, Charles Dotter.[1] Like many advances in medicine, Dotter's discovery was accidental. In 1963, he was passing a catheter into the main artery in the body to obtain X-ray pictures of the arteries to his patient's kidneys. By chance, as he passed the catheter, he opened up an as yet undiagnosed blockage in the artery to the patient's right leg. In January the following year, Dotter performed the first intentional angioplasty. His patient was Laura Shaw, an eighty-two-year-old woman with a painful gangrenous left foot. By opening up the artery in her thigh, Dotter was able to save her leg from being amputated.

This was not the first accidental discovery in radiology. In fact, the spe-cialty of radiology itself began with a chance breakthrough. In November of 1895, Wilhelm Roentgen was experimenting with cathode ray tubes. As luck would have it, he had left a piece of fluorescent material nearby and he no-ticed that the material glowed when the tube was switched on. He proposed that this effect was caused by a previously unknown kind of ray produced within the tube but passing through the glass of its walls. These rays, which could pass through some materials but not others, came to be called X-rays because "X" is a commonly used term for "unknown."

Roentgen's rays are still called X-rays today, even though science has long since worked out that they are a type of electromagnetic radiation on the same spectrum as light, microwaves, and radio waves. We know how X-rays are produced and how they interact with matter. Based on this knowledge, X-rays can be used safely for a great number of purposes, both medical and non-medical. In clinical practice, standardized techniques have been agreed upon for imaging different parts of the body. Contrast agents are used to highlight parts of the body that are not clearly seen on basic X-ray images. For some years, X-ray images were collected on photographic film but today the process is entirely digital, with the images displayed on computer screens. Once, I asked a new intake of medical students whether they had ever been X-rayed. The vast majority indicated yes. No wonder X-rays are considered to be one of the world's greatest scientific discoveries.

Cathode rays, like those Roentgen was studying, are in fact streams of electrons, and when fired at a metal object the electrons interact with the target to produce X-rays. As the electron slows down within the target, the energy is released as an X-ray. Alternatively, one of the accelerated elec-trons hits another electron within the target material, displacing it from

---

1. Payne, "Charles Theodore Dotter," 28.

the atom. An electron from further out in the atom moves down to fill the space and the excess energy is released as an X-ray. These processes can be readily understood by imagining the electrons are particles not unlike tiny billiard balls. But in certain experimental situations, the behavior of electrons becomes much more mysterious.

Electrons Are Particles and Waves

In the famous double-slit experiment, electrons are accelerated one at a time towards a target with two slits. Some electrons pass through one or other of the slits to hit a detector on the other side. It is easy to imagine that the electrons, acting like billiard balls, would pass through either slit and be detected at one of two positions on the detector depending on which slit they had passed through. In fact, when this experiment is done, it is just as likely that an electron will be detected in a third position mid-way between the two points that would be expected if electrons were particles.

This unexpected finding can be explained if electrons are thought of as waves. A single wave can pass through both slits, producing two separate waves on the other side. These waves interfere with each other, and the points where the waves cross are places where there is the highest probability of finding an electron. Each electron effectively passes through both slits at the same time. When electrons behave in this way, it is known as "quantum coherence."

It is now accepted that scientific observations about electrons can only be properly understood if electrons are indeed both particles and waves. Yet, a hundred years ago, the idea that anything could be both a particle and a wave would have been rejected as logically inconsistent. The recognition of the counterintuitive dual nature of electrons underlines an important principle concerning the scientific evaluation of evidence: *insights that are based on observations carry greater weight than conclusions made from first principles.*

This approach also exemplifies the way science looks to gather and weigh up an evidence base of experiences before attempting to put together broader interpretations.

Although atheists often celebrate science as a model for rational thinking, some arguments against the existence of God seem to ignore the scientific principle that places evidence before theory. One example is the Hiddenness Argument.

The Hiddenness of God

Something is stopping Harry from believing in God. He finds many aspects of Christianity attractive. He appreciates religious music and art and enjoys the Anglican service of Evensong in particular. Harry is not resistant to the idea of God but continues to have concerns about a range of intellectual issues related to faith. Take the Bible, for example. Why is it so hard to interpret? If God chooses to speak to us through Scripture, would he not make the text as unambiguous as possible? In short, Harry wonders why God's existence could not be more obvious. Perhaps, then, more people would be moved to worship him.

The Hiddenness Argument is based on the fact that it is all too easy to find people like Harry (although Harry himself is fictional). The line of reasoning broadly goes like this: If there is a God, he is perfectly loving. A perfectly loving God would wish to have a loving relationship with all his creatures. As a loving relationship cannot get started without believing the other party exists, God would make sure that all creatures capable of such a relationship would believe in his existence. However, there have been and still are people who do not believe in God but are not resistant to the idea of his existence. Therefore, a perfectly loving God does not exist.

This line of reasoning draws on two observations. First, God is experienced as loving. Second, God can be experienced as hidden. For Christianity, these dual experiences of God are readily identifiable in the Bible (see, for example, Psalm 136:1 and Romans 8:39 for God as loving, and Isaiah 45:15 and Psalm 10:1 for God as hidden). But rather than seeking to develop an understanding that can account for both observations, the Hiddenness Argument simply rejects them on account of their apparent internal contradiction. The argument therefore puts more weight on the principle of logical inconsistency than observation. Imagine if we were to apply the same approach to electrons. We might start by saying that if electrons exist, they must be particles. If electrons exist as particles, they will not have wave-like properties. Electrons can be observed as waves. Therefore, electrons do not exist.

This is clearly nonsense. The best way to interpret experimental evidence is to think of electrons as particles *and* waves, but this does not cause us to deny their existence. And if an electron can be both a particle and a wave, then God can be both loving and hidden. Just as electrons can be observed as waves or particles depending upon circumstances, people of faith sometimes experience God as loving, sometimes as hidden.

Although not repeatable at will in the way that experiments demonstrating the properties of electrons can be, these experiences display the three key characteristics outlined in chapter 2: they are sufficiently numerous as to be considered in serious theorizing, they form part of a network of interconnected experiences, and they have a corresponding impact on the lives of individuals and their communities.

Rather than being an argument for atheism, the apparent inconsistency between a loving God and a world in which people fail to recognize him represents a starting point for a deeper understanding. And a number of possible explanations for why God's existence is not more obvious have been proposed. One approach argues that God is not hidden, but some people are simply unable to properly interpret the evidence for his existence. Others consider God to be so far beyond human understanding that we are not in a position to make much sense of divine hiddenness. Alternatively, God may have good reasons for being less than obvious. For example, God may seek a particular kind of relationship that can only develop if we have the freedom to choose to believe or not. That freedom might not exist if God's presence were undeniable.

But if a loving God has reasons for being obscure, might he not let us know something about those reasons? And if the study of nature is one way to learn about the character of God, could there be clues to some of these reasons within the scientific record? Clearly, science alone can say nothing about the hiddenness of God, because the exclusion of the supernatural is a simplifying assumption fundamental to the scientific methodology. However, if we extend the scientific method by reinterpreting relevant research findings without the "Only Natural Causes" simplifying assumption, we can identify scientific studies that hint at possible explanations for divine hiddenness.

Uncertainty About God's Existence Promotes Survival of Religious Communities

In 2003, anthropologist Richard Sosis and psychologist Eric Bressler published the results of a study that compared the survival of religious and secular (i.e., non-religious) communes in the USA.[2] They found that secular communes were three times more likely to dissolve in a given year than religious ones. Because it was thought that rituals can promote cooperation

2. Sosis and Bressler, "Cooperation and Commune Longevity," 211–39.

between individuals, they looked to see whether communes with more rituals and constraints tended to last longer. At this point, they discovered significant differences in the impact of religious and secular rituals. More rituals and restraints were associated with longer survival for religious communes but not secular ones. They concluded that religious communes lasted longer because religious rituals and constraints are built on presuppositions that cannot be verified by logic, whereas secular rituals are based on "real-world" postulates that can be disproved.

The sense that God has concern for us as individuals is generally part of religious experience. But interpersonal relationship is also a strong feature of religious thought, in which God intends for us to follow a life of faith in community with others. A loving God would therefore desire the success of faith communities. The above research suggests that if God's existence were fully open to logical proof, there would be a negative impact on the survival of faith communities. On the other hand, by keeping his existence less obvious, God can seek a relationship with his people that is verified not only through reason but also physically and emotionally, for example through participation in religious rituals (see also part 2).

More Objective Evidence for God's Existence May Make no Difference

In 2013, cognitive psychologists Ara Norenzayan and Will Gervais conducted an extensive review of scientific studies into religious belief and behaviors.[3] They wanted to gather this research together into a general scheme that describes the mechanisms underlying religious disbelief. They identified four interacting pathways which can lead to religious disbelief. More than one pathway is likely to apply to any individual, and each combination of pathways will display different qualities.

Perhaps unsurprisingly, they concluded that argumentation is not the only factor behind religious disbelief. In fact, intellectual activity is involved in only one of the four pathways by which analytical thinking tends to block or overrule the intuitive processes that support belief in the supernatural. The other pathways describe people who experience an absence of intuitive support for personal gods, those with little or no motivation to find gods, and individuals who lack cultural support for belief in gods. Because evaluation of objective evidence is only relevant to the

3. Norenzayan and Gervais, "Origins of Religious Disbelief," 20–25.

analytical pathway, if any of the other pathways are significant for a given person, provision of additional evidence is unlikely to make any difference. In the words of Jesus, "neither will they be convinced if some one should rise from the dead" (Luke 16:31).

Making Decisions Despite Uncertainty

In chapter 2, we considered reasons why doctors often need to make decisions based on less-than-perfect evidence. Sometimes there are good reasons why the best evidence cannot be obtained. Likewise, there are good reasons why we should not expect to find the kind of evidence that would make it impossible to deny God's existence. Yet, other evidence is available to us, particularly the lived experiences that transform people of faith. And we too can be justified in basing decisions about God's existence on evidence of this sort.

The dual nature of electrons is related to the famous Heisenberg Uncertainty Principle. When an electron is like a particle, we can know its position but not the speed and direction of its motion. When it is a wave, we can know its speed and direction but not its position. Science has developed systems to handle this uncertainty. In the next chapter, we will see how science can offer a structured way for people of faith to deal with the uncertainty associated with God's hiddenness.

---------- 5 ----------

Faith and the Science of Uncertainty

MARGARET IS A SIXTY-EIGHT-YEAR-OLD retired science teacher. She has been unwell for several weeks, feeling hot with episodes of profuse sweating, particularly at night. She has taken her temperature during some of these episodes and found it to be between 100°F and 102°F (38°C and 39°C). But she has had no sites of pain. Margaret's GP has sent her into hospital for tests. Initial blood results suggested that there was a site of inflammation or infection somewhere in her body, but no bacteria had been found in her blood and a Computed Tomography body scan of Margaret's chest, abdomen, and pelvis was normal. The consultant in charge of Margaret's care has asked Mark, the junior doctor, to go to the medical imaging department to see if there are any other imaging tests that might show up a cause for the fevers. The duty consultant for nuclear medicine tells Mark there are three possible radioisotope tests that might help but, because Margaret's condition is relatively uncommon and medical imaging is a rapidly changing area, she will check the latest research to see which test would be the most effective.

The nuclear medicine consultant has recently read about a similar patient in a medical journal for whom a gallium scan had shown up a tumor as a cause for fevers, but at a conference earlier in the year, she also saw a presentation that suggested a newer test, FDG-PET, might be even better. However, she wants to do a more thorough check of the published literature. As she starts her search, a senior colleague walks in so, she asks his opinion.

"Which radioisotope test would you suggest for a case of pyrexia of unknown origin, John?" she asks.

"I haven't seen a case of PUO for some years, but based on my knowledge of the biology of inflammation and infection, I would recommend a radiolabeled white cell scan."

Her search of the literature finds a number of case studies in which the three tests were individually successful. But to do a proper comparison she needs to find studies in which at least two of the tests were performed in the same patients. She finds only two such studies, both comparing gallium scans to FDG-PET. Altogether, sixty patients were included. In both series, all causes for fevers identified by gallium scintigraphy were also detected by FDG-PET, but FDG-PET detected a cause in an additional eight cases. The literature search finds no studies comparing either of these tests to white cell scanning.

Based on the evidence above, what would *you* do if you were the nuclear medicine specialist?

- Take the advice of your senior colleague and recommend the patient should have a white cell scan.

- Recommend that the patient should have a gallium scan because it was successful in the case study.

- Recommend that the patient should undergo FDG-PET.

- Recommend that no radioisotope test would be appropriate for this patient as there is insufficient evidence to support the use of any of them.

Osler's Science of Uncertainty

An early experiment into the possible medical applications of X-rays involved taking an image of gallstones which had been inserted into a piece of beefsteak.[1] The stones were not visible on the images, but today we know that many gallstones do not contain enough calcium to be seen using standard X-ray techniques. The experiment was performed by one of the most influential physicians of all time, Sir William Osler (1849–1920). Osler was a Canadian physician who had been Regius Professor of Medicine at Oxford and co-founder of the Johns Hopkins Hospital in the USA. His name is particularly associated with a familial condition which causes repeated nosebleeds and small spidery red or purple clusters of blood

1. Lentle and Aldrich, "Radiological Sciences," 281.

vessels on the skin or in the lining of the mouth and other body cavities. The role of radiology in the diagnosis and treatment of this condition only became apparent after Osler's death, with the development of advanced X-ray techniques that could show abnormal blood vessels in deep organs such as the brain, lungs, and liver.

Osler is also known for his portrayal of medicine as a "science of uncertainty and an art of probability."[2] The scenario above illustrates that this maxim is just as true today. Uncertainty is an unavoidable part of medicine, and radiology is no exception. No diagnostic test is 100 percent accurate.

One problem with uncertainty is the potential it has to paralyze decision-making. Yet doctors in all branches of medicine need to commit to a course of action for their patients despite this uncertainty. Osler considered the acquisition and application of knowledge to be the key to the management of uncertainty and recommended that doctors should have "firm faith in a few, good well-tried drugs."[3] His approach laid the foundations for a methodology that is known today as evidence-based medicine, a concept that has been as important for demonstrating the safety and efficacy of X-rays and other diagnostic imaging tests as it has for medical treatments.

Evidence-based medicine entails the judicial use of the best available evidence. As an academic radiologist who performs imaging research, much of my work aims to add new information to this evidence base with the hope of further reducing uncertainty. Relevant evidence can come from multiple sources, and so an evidence-based framework has been established to help bring these different sources of information together in a coherent manner. The framework ranks the different types of evidence into levels, the lowest level being derived from first principles or expert opinion. For example, a statement that "this treatment ought to work because it is based on a particular medical principle" would count as low-level evidence. "I tried this treatment for a patient and it worked," would constitute a case study and would be one level higher. The highest level of evidence might comprise a systematic review of several studies in which patients were randomly assigned to one of two different treatments.

A key principle of evidence-based medicine is that there is no threshold level of evidence that should be obtained before making a decision for a particular patient. To require high-level evidence for every clinical decision would be unfair on a large number of patients, particularly those with rare

2. Bennett Bean, *Sir William Osler: Aphorisms*, 125.

3. Gomes and Haynes, "William Osler," 26.

diseases or unusual clinical circumstances where it has not been possible to undertake the research required to obtain high-level evidence. However, decisions should be made using the highest level of evidence available.

Evidence is strengthened if research findings agree across the different levels. For example, it would be inappropriate to select a treatment that seemed to be effective in a case study if higher levels of evidence indicated no benefit. On the other hand, it would be reasonable to use a case study as the basis for a decision for a similar patient if this were indeed the highest level of evidence available.

Uncertainty and Faith

Consider the following questions:

At this moment, is the number of pigeons in London's Trafalgar Square odd or even?

Which direction is this?

LEFT

Which of the following numbers is bigger?
3 or 5

Does God Exist?

The first three questions have one thing in common. Having no definite answer, they all bring about conflict and uncertainty in mental processing, and brain imaging has shown that when volunteers ponder these sorts of questions, a part of the brain known as the anterior cingulate gyrus becomes more active. More interestingly, the same part of the brain becomes active when people consider the last question, "Does the God of the Bible exist?" and this happens whether the subject believes in God or not. In other words, neuroscience suggests that reflecting on the question of God's existence engages the cognitive processes that deal with uncertainty.[4]

The current prominence of religious fundamentalism might give the impression that there is no room for uncertainty where belief in God is concerned. However, as author and commentator on religious affairs Karen

4. Harris et al., "Neural Correlates."

Armstrong highlights in her book, *The Case for God*, there is an equally strong, if not stronger, religious tradition that embraces the fact that knowledge of God is at best incomplete.[5] The notion that uncertainty is an unavoidable part of a commitment to God is reflected in spiritual practice. For example, the act of petitionary prayer in which God is asked for specific outcomes is based on an assumption that these outcomes are uncertain. By being willing to offer reasons for their faith, religious people are acknowledging that belief in God is something for debate rather than an indisputable fact. Within Christianity, uncertainty within the religious life is made explicit in Paul's letter to the Corinthians (1 Corinthians 13:12): "For now we see in a mirror dimly, but then face to face. Now I know in part; then I shall understand fully, even as I have been fully understood."

Experimental data has confirmed that uncertainty is common among people who are nevertheless committed to God. One survey of religious US subjects found that the majority acknowledged occasions of doubt about their religious faith, caused by evil in the world, perceived conflicts between faith and science, or the feeling that life really has no meaning.[6] But rather than being seen as undesirable, religious doubt has long been embraced as a route to developing a deeper and more meaningful faith. The medieval French scholastic philosopher, theologian, and logician Pierre Abélard (1079–1142) is quoted as saying, "The beginning of wisdom is found in doubting; by doubting we come to the question, and by seeking we may come upon the truth." Moreover, research data suggests that coping with religious doubt in a positive way may avoid the adverse effects on health that can result from negative approaches to religious uncertainty.

Faith, Worship, and the Science of Uncertainty

When Osler talked about having faith in a few drugs, by no means did he mean that doctors should use them despite or because of a lack of evidence that they worked. Quite the opposite, in fact. Just as the acquisition and application of knowledge is key to the management of uncertainty in medicine, the same can be said of the uncertainty that is an inevitable part of religion. But we can go further and adapt the scientific principles of evidence-based medicine to religious uncertainty. Faith can also be a science of uncertainty. The aim would not be to prove God's existence, but

5. Armstrong, *Case for God.*
6. Krauseal and Ellison, "Doubting Process."

to provide a framework in which people of faith can provide others with reasons for their belief (see 1 Peter 3:15), and to provide a positive way to deal with religious uncertainty, especially if this uncertainty arises from a perceived conflict between faith and science.

Faith and worship are closely linked. The way we believe in God affects the way we worship, and vice versa. An evidence-based approach to faith can generate a correspondingly structured motivation for worship. As documented in the Bible (Matthew 28:17), doubt and worship can co-exist. By allowing religious uncertainty about God to be managed in a positive way, an evidence-based framework for the evaluation of spiritual experiences can enable a fuller engagement with worship, even in the presence of doubt. However, just as evidence-based medicine does not encompass the whole interaction between patient and doctor, the proposed evidence-based approach to faith and worship should be complemented by other approaches to knowledge of God which reflect the interpersonal nature of the relationship between God and humankind.

The Evidence Pyramid

In evidence-based medicine, a pyramid diagram was created to help us understand how to weigh different levels of evidence. We can develop a similar diagram for a systematic approach to evidence that includes lived experiences that are not obtainable at will, using the principles outlined in previous chapters. The pyramid is divided into levels, with the highest level of evidence at the top and the lowest at the bottom. As we go up the levels, we can be more confident about interpretations drawn from that evidence. Although conclusions should be based on the highest level of evidence available, as discussed in chapter 2, it is not necessary to have the highest possible level of evidence, especially when there are valid reasons why such evidence might not be available. We can also borrow another important principle from evidence-based medicine: consistency across different levels adds weight to evidence.

The highest level of evidence (level 1) is provided by experimental data that can be independently verified. This is the paradigm of scientific enquiry. As outlined in chapter 1, when interpreting experimental data, it is essential to identify underlying assumptions and to consider how different assumptions might affect the interpretation of results (e.g., the No God Assumption).

The next three levels below are grouped into a block that comprises evidence from lived experiences that cannot be obtained at will and cannot therefore be independently verified in the same way as experimental data. The levels within this group are weighted using standardized criteria developed in chapter 2, namely they: a) are sufficiently common to be worthy of inclusion in serious theorizing, b) form part of a network of interconnected experiences and theories, and c) have corresponding lasting effects on the life of the individual and the community in which they live. Experiences that meet all three criteria fall into level 2. Level 3 will comprise experiences that demonstrate only two of these characteristics, including individual experiences that *both* form part of a network of interconnected experiences and theories, *and* have corresponding lasting effects on the life of the individual and the community in which they live. Lived experiences that meet only one criterion will make up level 4.

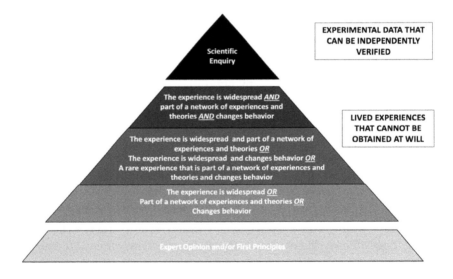

Figure 2. Evidence-based pyramid that incorporates lived experiences unobtainable at will

Expert opinion and evidence derived only from first principles are assigned the lowest level of evidence (level 5), as is the case for evidence-based medicine. This level will include evidence grounded solely on philosophical or scientific principles without corresponding data gained from lived experiences (regardless of whether the experience is obtainable on demand or not). As we will see in chapter 7, purely philosophical arguments become even more problematic if human reasoning is considered to have arisen from evolution natural selection alone. In the words of the American philosopher Thomas M. Crisp, "If you are a sophisticated atheist or agnostic and your only grounds for this are philosophical . . . then your atheism (agnosticism) is poorly grounded."[7] Although focusing on the argument from evil, Crisp points out that his statement applies equally to other arguments for the non-existence of God, such as the argument from divine hiddenness (chapter 4) and the multiverse hypothesis (chapter 6).

An evidence-based commitment to God will entail the conscientious and judicious use of current best evidence to evaluate claims about God. Evidence will not only relate to God's existence but also his character, purposes, and relationship with the natural world and humanity. As outlined in chapter 1, scientific data can be reinterpreted from a perspective that allows for God's existence. Therefore, all levels of evidence are potentially relevant.

Lived Experience and Divine Revelation

Lived experiences that disclose God's reality or purposes are sometimes termed as "divine revelation." These experiences may have no apparent stimulus or can be brought about by an encounter with someone else, by an awareness of nature, or by engaging with religious texts. An experience of this sort is not always overtly religious but could be a "limit experience," described by Canadian Philosopher Charles Taylor as "an experience which unsettles and breaks through our ordinary sense of being in the world, with its familiar objects, activities and points of reference."[8]

The former Archbishop of Canterbury, Rowan Williams, has also written about the disruptive character of an experience of God, describing how it can shake our self-image such that we may no longer recognize ourselves. Encounters with God can produce an odd mixture of insight and disquiet, of elation and loss. In a description that echoes some of the early responses to X-rays, he writes:

7. Crisp, "Evolutionary Objection," 132.
8. McPherson, "Re-Enchanting the World," 176.

God's "ray" cuts through our blindness and ignorance; it cuts through something as beams of light do. God is "the light of the world" in his Son Jesus, yet that interruption, that light cutting through our darkness, is not a comfortable clearing up of problems and smoothing out of our difficulties and upsets. On the contrary . . . when God's light breaks on my darkness, the first thing I know is that I don't know, and never did.[9]

Williams highlights the importance of such encounters for Christian thinking, but they are not simply random events. One particular historical community went through experiences of this kind with increasing intensity until it reached a crisis point that deeply challenged the way people thought about God and themselves. And into this community came one particular man whose words and actions revealed an exceptional closeness to God, even as he suffered "the terrified violence of those who couldn't cope with God and themselves." For Christians, he *is* "that which interrupts and disturbs and remakes the world."[10]

One question that is rarely addressed when considering experiences of God is how these encounters occur. It has been proposed that the way we obtain knowledge of God through lived experience is similar to how we gain knowledge of the past, or of objects in our immediate surroundings. Indeed, scientific studies of religious experiences suggest that comparable mental processes are involved. But there is still the question of how a supernatural being can influence the natural biological processes that underpin human responses to God. An ability to point to possible mechanisms for these interactions would add significant weight to the evidence provided by lived experiences of God. Possible mechanisms are discussed in detail in part 2.

Evidence from Religious Texts

Religious texts are a cornerstone for a commitment to God and they can be considered as evidence at multiple levels. Some parts, specifically those that are historical, will constitute level 1 evidence that can be independently verified. This would include, for example, the historical actuality of Jesus, which is considered certain by virtually all scholars of Christianity, believers or otherwise. Historical evidence is of fundamental importance

9. Williams, *Ray of Darkness*, 100.
10. Williams, *Ray of Darkness*, 103.

to a commitment to God but, in view of the scientific focus of this book, it will not be considered in detail.

A major part of religious texts consists of accounts of lived experiences of God, and these will fall within levels 2–4, depending on how they meet the three criteria described above. These accounts will have been selected for inclusion within the body of religious texts because they form part of an interconnected network of experiences and theories about the nature of God. Many will describe experiences of God that have had corresponding lasting effects on the life of the individual and the community in which they live.

But there is another way in which religious texts can provide evidence. They can function as "laboratory notes" that describe how experiences which provide evidence can be created for oneself. By reading or listening to their content and engaging with the narratives, the reader or listener can gain a personal sense of what an interaction with God may be like. Such texts can be considered "mythical" in the sense that they possess deep power and symbolic meaning, and the account need not necessarily be factually accurate to serve this function. This approach accords with that outlined by C. S. Lewis in his *Reflections on the Psalms*, where he writes that we encounter God in Scripture "by not using it as an encyclopaedia or encyclical but by steeping ourselves in its tone and temper and so learning its overall message."[11] When experiences gained in this way are sufficiently common and have corresponding effects on the lives and communities of those undergoing them, they can be considered as level 2 evidence.

In medical dramas on television or in films, X-ray images are frequently displayed back to front or upside down. And there is no reason to expect production staff to know which way X-rays should be displayed. Similarly, most people would not expect to be able to recognize particular diseases on an X-ray, or understand some of the terms, such as "septal lines" or "silhouette sign," which a specialist medical practitioner proficient in interpreting medical images (i.e., a radiologist) might use to describe certain appearances. A wide range of abilities is required to interpret X-rays, not least a knowledge of the anatomy displayed, the disease processes that can affect the organ under evaluation, and physics of how the image is produced. No wonder it takes twelve to fifteen years to become a radiologist.

But when it comes to religious texts, some people seem to expect to be able to interpret them with little or no training. Some comments that

---

11. Lewis, *Reflections on the Psalms*, 88.

prominent atheists have made about the Bible, for instance, show about as much expertise as someone who displays an X-ray upside down. Misreading the seemingly negative characteristics of God as described in the Old Testament is a common example. I do not claim to have highly developed skills in biblical interpretation, but if the Bible is seen as a database of experiences of God, it does not take much interpretive ability to see that these passages may not be a description of God's actual character, but reflections on how an experience of God can sometimes feel. Other texts will show how to deal effectively with such feelings.

By way of example, consider the biblical book of Job, which co-president of the Freedom from Religion Foundation Dan Barker includes in a list of ten worst Old Testament verses, passages he considers to affirm Richard Dawkins' assertion that God is a capriciously malevolent bully. And the book of Job certainly seems to portray God negatively. God appears to play games with the life of his blameless servant Job. Satan tricks God into allowing him complete freedom in his attack on Job. Job's children are sacrificed so that God can prove that nothing will change Job's commitment to God.

When looked at as an experience of God, the story of Job can be seen as a description of how sometimes it can feel as though God is behind this suffering. Bad things happen to innocent people, and how can we reconcile this with a loving God? The ability of the book of Job to create a first-hand experience of God can be seen by looking at the book as a thought experiment, as proposed by philosopher and theologian Yiftach Fehige. As we have already seen in chapter 1, experiments may require the adoption of assumptions that are not necessarily true and Fehige points out how this also applies to thought experiments. With Job, the thought experiment provides opportunities for learning something new by asking the question, "What if God were the cause of suffering?"[12]

Early chapters in the book of Job explore potential explanations for undeserved suffering, starting from an assumption that God lies behind this suffering in some way. Perhaps God does not govern the natural world properly, for example. However, none of these explanations succeeds, and we are therefore forced to abandon the starting assumption and consider alternative interpretations. In the final part of the book, God eventually responds with an interesting answer. He points out the severe limitations of human knowledge, but, rather than refer to humanity's poor grasp of metaphysics

12. Fehige, "Book of Job as a Thought Experiment."

or philosophy, God provides a long list of things about nature that humans cannot explain. The implication is that if you want to understand the relationship between God and suffering, you need to understand nature.

From the above analysis, we can see that the book of Job is much more nuanced than a simple statement of what should be believed. But how does it address the problem of suffering? Christian physicist and Fellow of the Royal Society, Tom Mcleish, offers an interpretation of Job that can take us some of the way towards answering the problem of suffering. He explains how the human lack of understanding of nature reflects a broken relationship between humanity and the natural world, and it is this that lies behind suffering. Nature hurts us and we hurt nature. Knowledge of the natural world can help heal this disconnection. Rather than portraying God as a malevolent bully, it turns out the book of Job points to a God who encourages us to do the science which many atheists hold in such high regard.[13]

The biblical passages cited in this book aim to provide experiential data in support of the point under discussion. Often, the text itself records an event that was experienced by only a small number of people. However, these accounts have also triggered experiences of God in many others, so that a widespread experience has been brought about with the passage of time. These experiences form part of an interconnected set of related experiences and theories that are associated with an observable change in behavior. The quoted passages are therefore offered as level 2 evidence.

Scripture and Science

The question of how to relate Scripture and science is by no means new. For instance, in his book, *The Literal Meaning of Genesis*, theologian and philosopher St Augustine (354–430) wrote:

> If they find a Christian mistaken in a field which they themselves know well and hear him maintaining foolish opinions about our books, how are they going to believe those books in matters concerning the resurrection of the dead, the hope of eternal life, and the kingdom of heaven, when they think their pages are full of falsehoods on facts which they have learnt from experience and the light of reason?[14]

---

13. McLeish, *Faith and Wisdom in Science*.

14. Augustine, *Literal Meaning of Genesis*, 42–43.

Passages such as this point to a long tradition within Christianity that seeks to align Scripture and secular knowledge of the natural world (which we would know today as science), even if this requires a reinterpretation of religious texts. This way of thinking is consistent with the evidence pyramid described above which places more weight on experiences that are obtainable on demand over the database of lived experiences contained within Scripture. Augustine also made a distinction between evidence and theory, giving more weight to Scripture than theory, paralleling the low weight given to interpretations based on first principles alone in the evidence pyramid outlined in this chapter:

> When they are able, from reliable evidence, to prove some fact of physical science, we shall show that it is not contrary to our Scripture. But when they produce from any of their books a theory contrary to Scripture, and therefore contrary to the Catholic faith, either we shall have some ability to demonstrate that it is absolutely false, or at least we ourselves will hold it without a shadow of a doubt.[15]

Nevertheless, those who interpret the Bible literally may find this view challenging because, for example, one would have to accept the age of the earth as being approximately 4.5 billion years as opposed to values of less than 10,000 years that are implied by Scripture. Yet prioritizing scientific data over biblical descriptions of the natural world can be justified in a number of ways. First, we should recognize that the Bible was never intended to be a book of natural history. Historical study has shown that the creation story in Genesis has many features in common with creation stories from other contemporary cultures. These stories were in effect the cosmology of the time. The writers of Genesis can be seen as reinterpreting this cosmology from the standpoint of a new religious perspective, that of commitment to only one God.

Second, investigation of the natural world is the study of God's creation and therefore a valid way to gaining knowledge of God. Science now tells us that the universe started with the big bang. Like the writers of Genesis in their day, we can reinterpret this modern cosmology from a faith perspective. Indeed, the big bang clearly resonates with the Judeo–Christian notion of God creating the universe. We can apply this approach to scientific data more generally, and when level 1 evidence and religious texts agree, the weight of evidence is increased.

15. Augustine, *Literal Meaning of Genesis*, 42–43.

Sometimes, re-evaluating Scripture in the light of new scientific data can create theological difficulties. For example, some features of the natural world, such as plate tectonics and evolution by natural selection, are associated with death and suffering. To accept that these processes occurred before humanity's estrangement from God (as represented in the Genesis story of Adam) might raise the question of why a loving God would use such harmful processes to create the world. Solutions to difficulties of this sort have been proposed, as touched on in the next chapter.

Using the Evidence Pyramid

A scientific style of thought seeks to develop and evaluate an evidence base of experiences before attempting to formulate wider forms of understanding. The evidence pyramid embraces this approach, which contrasts with the presentation of religious knowledge as "handed down from God" and hence unquestionable. The system is therefore likely to be better suited to scientifically minded individuals. Accordingly, use of the evidence pyramid will begin with experience rather than theory.

The starting point will often be experiences that are obtainable at will (i.e., level 1 evidence), but comprising data for which there are competing interpretations depending on the underlying assumptions. In this situation, we can look to see how each interpretation is supported by lower levels of evidence, reflecting the principle that consistency across different levels adds weight to evidence. Accordingly, evidence based on semi-experimental data (experience unobtainable at will; levels 2–4) will become significant, having priority over evidence based on first principles or expert opinion (level 5).

For some questions, it may not be possible to identify relevant level 1 evidence. In this case, the analysis will start with the highest level of evidence available (ideally level 2). Consistency with lower levels will again come into play if there are competing interpretations based on level 2 data.

The evidence pyramid cannot be used to assemble proofs for the existence of God because there will always be uncertainty when using semi-experimental data (levels 2–4). However, the pyramid can show how evidence based on lived experiences of God can contribute to an individual's commitment to God, despite this uncertainty. This evidence-based approach may also stimulate others to give more serious consideration to the possibility of God's existence.

The Great Cop-out?

Richard Dawkins has said that "Faith is the great cop-out, the great excuse to evade the need to think and evaluate evidence."[16] Noticeably, he offers no evidence to support this statement. The approach to grading evidence proposed above is clearly not open to this criticism and is consistent with a more accurate definition of faith as commitment despite uncertainty. Looked at in this way, faith works alongside a rational evaluation of evidence. A comprehensive evaluation of the evidence for and against the existence of God should include all forms of evidence. Surely the great cop-out is the uncritical and groundless evasion of the need to evaluate evidence based on lived experiences, even if they cannot be obtained at will? The belief that only natural properties and causes exist is based on a partial evaluation of evidence, and to paraphrase Christopher Hitchens, that which is asserted on partial evidence can be dismissed on partial evidence.[17]

But what about Margaret? We will hear more of her story in the next chapter.

16. Dawkins, Speech at the Edinburgh International Science Festival.
17. Hitchens, *God Is Not Great*, 150.

6

Faith, Evidence, and the Multiverse

MARGARET IS RADIOACTIVE. THE nuclear medicine specialist recommended a PET scan as the best way to find the cause of her fevers. Arun, the nuclear medicine technologist, has just injected a small amount of a radioactive substance into her arm. "Radioactive sugar," was how Arun described it. "It will go to any sites of inflammation or other possible causes for fever that are active in your body and show up on the scan we will do later." Margaret is not sure she likes the idea of being radioactive.

"Will I glow in the dark?" she asked the doctor who had explained the procedure to her. The doctor said that she would not, but in any case, everybody is slightly radioactive. This is because radioactive substances created in the stars of the early universe were spread around the cosmos when those stars exploded at the end of their lives. Some of this material became mixed with the matter that formed the Earth. It is still around today and gets taken into the human body. It seems we are all made of stardust.

Margaret's scan showed up inflammation within the aorta, a major blood vessel in her chest. She was diagnosed with vasculitis and started on treatment with anti-inflammatory steroid tablets. Her fevers stopped and she felt much better. A repeat PET scan performed three months later showed that the inflammation had resolved.

PET stands for Positron Emission Tomography. The radioisotope Margaret was given emits a subatomic particle known as a positron or positive electron. When this positron encounters a nearby electron, the two particles are annihilated and the matter is turned into energy in the form of gamma photons emitted in opposite directions. The PET scanner detects these photons and creates an image of where the radioactivity is located within the body.

Intriguingly, theoretical physicist Paul Dirac had proposed the existence of the positron before its reality could be confirmed by experiment. He deduced that the positron should exist based on an equation. And this is just one of many instances where mathematics has predicted a feature of the natural world prior to its observation by scientific testing. These occurrences highlight the remarkable concordance between mathematical theory and the behavior of the physical world. But why should mathematics be so effective in describing the natural world? It is hard, if not impossible, to provide an explanation from the standpoint of science alone—at best, it can only be seen as an unlikely coincidence. But this conformity is so much more understandable if one believes the physical universe is grounded on the rationality of God. In his book *God's Undertaker: Has Science Buried God?* Christian mathematician John Lennox points out that it is "not surprising when the mathematical theories spun by human minds created in the image of God's Mind, find ready application in a universe whose architect was that same creative Mind."[1]

Physical Constants

The mathematical equations describing the processes involved in positron emission are complex but involve a quantity known as the fine structure constant, introduced by the German theoretical physicist Arnold Sommerfeld in 1916. At the time, he was working at the University of Munich, having been appointed to this position by Wilhelm Roentgen, the discoverer of X-rays. Sommerfeld's doctoral students included many famous physicists contributing to the field of quantum physics, including Werner Heisenberg and Wolfgang Pauli. The fine structure constant is one of a range of physical quantities that are believed to be unchanging throughout the universe, and Margaret's scan would not have been possible if this quantity were very different from its value of $1/137$. The radioactive sugar may have decayed too quickly or too slowly to be useful for imaging, or perhaps not been radioactive at all. Then again, with a different value for the fine structure constant, there would be no life on Earth.

All matter is made of elementary particles, some of which carry an electrical charge (specifically protons, electrons, and positrons). These elementary charged particles interact with electromagnetic fields. Sommerfeld's equation states that the strength of these interactions is fixed, as characterized

1. Lennox, *God's Undertaker*, 61.

by the fine structure constant, α. The strength of coupling between elementary charged particles and electromagnetic fields is fundamental to a wide range of natural phenomena, such as chemical reactions, the production of X-rays, and radioactivity. In certain types of radioactive decay, charged particles are ejected from the atomic nucleus, and this process will be influenced by electromagnetic interactions. The value of the fine structure constant will therefore determine the likelihood that a particular chemical element will be radioactive as well as the speed at which it decays.

Radioactivity is often thought of as sinister and dangerous. However, if used responsibly, radioactive substances can be very effective for diagnosing and treating a variety of diseases, as illustrated by Margaret's story. Radioactive processes were also crucial for bringing about an Earth that has conditions compatible with life. For example, iron atoms resulting from radioactive decay processes within the first stars were later incorporated into the Earth's core. This iron generates the Earth's magnetic field which in turn protects the Earth's atmosphere from being stripped away by the stream of charged particles released from the Sun, known as the solar wind. If the fine structure constant had a different value, there would be drastically less iron in the Earth.

Other substances incorporated into the fabric of the Earth continue to undergo radioactive decay today, producing significant amounts of heat in the process. Without this heat, the Earth would have cooled too quickly to allow for the development of complex life forms. It is also recognized that the development of life on Earth required a planet with a rigid outer shell formed of plates that move on a liquid-like layer immediately below. The movement of these plates, known as plate tectonics, is driven by the Earth's heat, including heat generated by radioactive decay. This process also causes new material to rise to the Earth's surface, bringing the chemical components required for life. It may be perplexing to know that volcanoes and earthquakes are in effect by-products of a process that is essential for the development and maintenance of life. But for all this to happen, the Earth must produce just the right amount of heat. Too little heat and the crust would be too thick to move; too much and the surface itself would be molten and unsuitable for life. Recent calculations show that variations in the fine structure constant as small as 6 percent would alter radioactive rates of decay sufficiently to stop the development of life from happening.[2]

2. Sandora, "Fine Structure Constant."

The fine structure constant is just one of twenty-six similar fixed physical quantities that characterize the properties of elementary particles and their interactions. Calculations like those described above have been performed for all of them, and small changes in just a few, or sometimes only one, of these constants would result in a universe that could not sustain life. Some hypothetical universes would exist for only a brief moment. There are others in which chemical bonds are impossible, or where atoms or stars cannot exist. The chance that the exact combination of values found in our life-bearing universe would occur is vanishingly small, so small that scientists have found it difficult to convey just how improbable our universe is. Physicist Paul Davies has likened the accuracy required to firing a bullet and hitting a one-inch target on the other side of the universe, twenty billion light years away.[3] Our universe appears to be very finely tuned indeed!

The Significance of Fine-tuning

How should we respond to the suggestion that we may be living on a rare planet in a very special universe? If we limit our analysis to observable scientific data alone, we can simply accept that the fine-tuning of the universe is a lucky coincidence. It is just the way things are, and had they been otherwise, no one would be here to see it. For many, this way of thinking is too passive given the extraordinary degree of fine-tuning shown by science.

Another approach is to suggest that our universe is just one of a vast collection of universes, each with differing physical properties. As luck would have it, our universe happens to have the correct characteristics to allow for the emergence of life. Although there is no direct evidence that other universes exist, the existence of multiple universes can be postulated using established theories about the expansion of the universe and quantum mechanics.

If we interpret the apparent fine-tuning of the universe within a framework that allows for a reality that extends beyond nature, it is readily explained by the existence of a fine-tuner—the creator God. Encountering and worshipping God as creator are core features of religious faith, and the feelings of awe and wonder inspired by the natural world frequently underlie such experiences. Rather than being a single act at a particular moment in time, God's creative activity is seen as continuous, such that the natural world is in every moment dependent upon him for its existence.

3. Davies, *God and the New Physics*, 179.

God as creator is a key component of a network of related experiences and theories. For instance, God as creator links to a fundamental aspect of Christian teaching (also found in other religions), that humans bear the image of God (Genesis 1:27). This concept signifies a connection between God and humanity such that humans have certain qualities in common with God, allowing him to become apparent in the world. Human creativity is therefore seen as a reflection of God's creativity. And recognition of God as creator is associated with changes in behavior, perhaps most notably in the form of worship.

Bad Tuning?

But there is another set of observations that needs to be fitted in within the notion of a creator God. Some of the features of the natural world that appear to be important for the development of life have side effects that lead to suffering. For example, the heat of the earth is linked to earthquakes, which are considered to have accounted for half of the ten most deadly natural disasters since 1900. Why would a God of love create a universe in which there are natural disasters such as earthquakes and volcanoes? Is this a case of bad tuning?

The network of experiences and theories associated with the concept of God as creator also acknowledges that humans do not have the capacity for a complete understanding of God. We cannot expect to comprehend fully the rationale behind divine actions. Nevertheless, some have suggested that adverse events of this kind might be understood as unfortunate yet unavoidable by-products of a creative freedom which God has conferred on his creation. This freedom has allowed intelligent life to emerge and ultimately enter willingly into relationship with him. To some, this explanation may seem inadequate, given the amount of suffering and death involved. At this point, it is worth noting that the multiverse hypothesis does not remove this difficulty. In fact, the problem is considerably amplified because similar effects on living beings are likely to occur within several universes.

The Christian experience of God entails an acknowledgment that humans are inclined to reject God. It is conceivable that God may have anticipated the human predisposition to promote self over relationship with him, and fashioned his creation accordingly. The same radioactive elements that provide the internal heat of the Earth have been used by humankind to create terrible weapons of mass destruction. Perhaps even more devastating outcomes could be envisaged were humans to reject God in an alternative universe with physical properties that precluded natural disasters. In other words, some of the adverse characteristics within nature may be tolerated by a loving God because they reduce the negative effects that would occur should he be rejected by humans (or perhaps other sentient beings elsewhere in the universe). Despite its negative features, the universe in which we live may have also presented the lowest possible chance that humans would reject God in the first place. Furthermore, certain aspects of nature that seem to be undesirable to us today may ultimately provide the means to bring about a universe that will compensate for the existing negative features.

A universe that is very different in character from the one we currently inhabit does form part of Christian thinking. Unlike the multiple independent universes hypothesized by some scientists, the alternative universe of Christianity is brought about by the transformation of the existing one, a process that will bring not only humanity but also the whole of creation into a new state of being and relationship with God. Setting right the death and suffering that is integral to our existing world is part of this vision of hope. The Bible likens the suffering that is part of the current creation to the pains of childbirth (Romans 8:22), as nature gets ready for its forthcoming transformation.

Recent advances in physics also point to a distinct possibility that at some point in the future, the universe could transition into a new state. This process would involve a transformation not unlike that seen with certain radioactive nuclei which decay by changing their energy state. The white cell scan which the nuclear specialist considered among the possible investigations for Margaret's fevers uses such an isotope, known as technetium-99m. The "m" stands for metastable, reflecting the excited higher energy state of the nucleus. In a given time period, there is a defined probability that the nucleus will shift to the stable state, releasing the excess energy as a gamma ray. The imaging equipment detects these gamma rays, showing where the white cells have accumulated in the patient's body.

The metastable component of the universe is the Higgs field, which is a field of energy that exists throughout the cosmos. When an elementary particle such as an electron passes through the field, it gains mass by interacting with another particle associated with the field, known as the Higgs boson. If the Higgs field is metastable, the energy of the field could shift at any moment to a lower value, in which case all subatomic particles such as electrons, neutrons, and protons would acquire completely new mass values. This event would alter the way subatomic particles attract one another and even change the force of gravity. The new universe would certainly be very different from the one we have now.

As discussed in previous chapters, we can initially interpret the apparent fine-tuning of the universe using the "Only Natural Causes" simplifying assumption, excluding semi-experimental data based on experience unobtainable at will. But an unbiased evaluation of the evidence also requires us to consider how our interpretation would be affected by allowing for the existence of God, incorporating semi-experimental data. We can also compare the two analyses using the evidence pyramid described in the previous chapter.

The apparent fine-tuning of the universe is based on observations that are repeatable at will and therefore comprise level 1 evidence. The multiverse hypothesis can be considered as level 5 evidence because there are no direct observations of other universes, and if they did exist, it is hard to see how they could be accessible to scientific study. The multiverse hypothesis is derived from first principles alone, specifically quantum mechanics and expansion theory. The notion of multiple universes hardly seems to comply with a key scientific principle known as Occam's razor—i.e., when selecting between competing explanations for the same occurrence, the one that requires the least speculation is usually correct. With the evidence-based approach described, lower-level evidence is to be accepted if no other evidence is available. Under such circumstances, it may be reasonable to accept the multiverse hypothesis.

But when we remove the assumptions that nothing exists beyond nature and include evidence gained from experiences unobtainable at will, we come to an entirely different conclusion. Experiences of God as creator are extremely widespread and sufficiently common to be included in serious theorizing, being documented in multiple cultures and over extended periods of time. They are also associated with long-term changes in behavior—for example, worship. These experiences therefore constitute level 2 evidence and offer an understanding of the fine-tuning of the universe that has greater weight of evidence than the multiverse hypothesis (level 5). This does not prove the existence of God because there will always be some uncertainty when using semi-experimental (level 2) data. However, the analysis illustrates how the fine-tuning of the universe can contribute to an individual's decision to commit to God despite uncertainty. It also suggests that the existence of a creator God is worthy of serious consideration as a better alternative to the multiverse hypothesis, and one that offers deeper insights into the natural world.

7

Faith and Reason

MAJOR SCIENTIFIC ADVANCES OFTEN start with seemingly simple questions, like the one asked by English electrical engineer Sir Godfrey Hounsfield and radiologist Jamie Ambrose: Is it possible to work out the contents of a box by taking multiple X-ray pictures in different positions around the object? Their solutions to the problem led to the development of the medical imaging technique known as Computed Tomography (CT, often called a CAT scan). Starting their work in the late 1960s, their main aim was to create images of the brain. In those days, other X-ray techniques could provide relatively little information about the brain because the surrounding skull bone tended to obscure the tissues within. In 1979, Hounsfield shared the Nobel Prize for medicine with Allan MacLeod Cormack, who had been performing similar work in the USA.

There is a well-known story about one of the early experiments undertaken by Hounsfield and Ambrose when developing the CT scanner. Initial tests of the device using human brains which had been preserved in chemical formalin had been unsuccessful. Looking for something that was closer to a living brain, they tried scanning a cow's head from a butcher's shop. Disappointingly, the images showed none of the details of the brain anatomy they had hoped to see. Ambrose suggested that maybe the blow to the head used to kill the cow had destroyed the brain structure. So they repeated the experiment with a cow's head obtained from a kosher butcher where the animal had been killed by blood-letting. On this occasion, the CT scan showed the brain anatomy with beautiful clarity.

If you are finding this discussion about the brain uncomfortable, you may be one of the many people who experience disgust when shown images of internal organs. In the early years after the discovery of X-rays, many people were horrified by being able to see the skeleton of a living person. Even in recent decades, the emotional impact of seeing inside the body has been exploited in public health campaigns.[1] But it is hard to pin down why people may feel disgust when seeing or hearing about internal organs. It is thought that disgust evolved as a way of protecting ourselves from exposure to infection or poisons, but this clearly does not apply when observing bodily organs. One influential theory suggests that, in these circumstances, disgust is more psychological or philosophical than physical. It is about protecting the way we view our bodies and minds. The discomfort we feel when viewing internal organs arises because we are reminded that humans are just biological entities rather than the advanced, rational, mind-based people we prefer to think we are.

Some people seem to find the idea of worshipping God distasteful, or even disgusting, for seemingly similar reasons. They view faith as a violation of our rational nature. Francis Crick, co-discoverer of the structure of DNA, once said that his research for a purely chemical basis for life was driven by his distaste for religion. The New Atheists are particularly inclined to deride belief in God as primitive and irrational. See, for example, the words of writer Christopher Hitchens: "Religion . . . comes from the bawling and fearful infancy of our species, and is a babyish attempt to meet our inescapable demand for knowledge (as well as for comfort, reassurance, and other infantile needs)."[2]

At first glance, the mental images triggered by the words used to describe God, especially within Christianity, can seem primitive, coming from a time when no one had the smallest idea of what the universe was really like. Even today, in many Christian churches you will hear people say they believe that God had a "Son," apparently not unlike mythical beings such as Zeus of Poseidon. They speak about how the "Son" "descended to the dead," as though there were a separate land under the surface of the earth. Later, the "Son" is said to have "ascended into heaven" to be "seated at the right hand of the Father," as though he occupies a special chair in the sky. How could anyone sign up to this concept of reality which centuries of scientific discovery have shown to be false?

In many ways, mental images of God are similar to X-ray images of the human body. In both cases, our pictures are incomplete. Take, for example, a CT scan of the brain. If you compare an actual brain to a corresponding CT

---

1. Lupton, "Revolting Bodies."
2. Hitchens, *God Is Not Great*, 64.

image, you might notice several differences. First, the CT image is displayed in shades of grey. The colored features of the real brain, such as blood vessels, are therefore less obvious. On closer inspection, you would see that the real brain has darker areas towards the edges with lighter areas just inside. The darker areas are the grey matter, while the lighter areas comprise the white matter. However, there is an opposite appearance on the CT scan: the grey matter is displayed in a lighter shade of grey than the white matter. This is because the white matter contains more fat, which blocks X-rays less than the water within the grey matter. Although CT images do not provide an entirely accurate picture of the brain, they are still extremely useful.

Perhaps there are other imaging techniques that can depict the brain more accurately? Magnetic resonance imaging was developed after CT, and this technique can show the grey matter as darker than white matter. But then the skull is shown as black, not white as in reality.

In fact, there are several ways to scan the brain, but each of them creates images that are like a real brain in some respects but unlike it in others. The complexity of the brain is never fully captured. Despite these limitations, these images are invaluable for brain research and the care of patients with brain diseases, not least because, unless the skull is opened surgically, the brain cannot be seen in any other way. Nevertheless, these images can be essential for making decisions about patients. The fact that doctors use brain images which are only partially accurate does not mean they have an inadequate understanding of the brain.

Professor of Medical Education, John McLachlan, and colleagues have suggested that, except for brain surgeons and pathologists, most doctors may not need to know what a real brain looks like. They could learn all they need to know about brain anatomy from medical imaging, despite the inevitable differences between these scans and a real brain. Their training includes knowing the limitations of the scans they use.[3] And we can ask whether people of faith are in a similar position. Perhaps they are equally aware of the limitations of the seemingly outmoded and unscientific mental images of God they use.

In his book *Miracles*, C. S. Lewis points out that the limitations of the mental images used by Christians were realized from very early on.[4] For example, we can find in the Bible representations of God as having human like characteristics. He appeared to Ezekiel as "a likeness as it were of a

3. McLachlan et al., "Teaching Anatomy Without Cadavers."

4. Lewis, *Miracles*, 93.

human form" (Ezekiel 1:26). But Deuteronomy 4:15–16 warns about the dangers of visualizing God in this way: "Since you saw no form on the day that the Lord spoke to you at Horeb out of the midst of the fire, beware lest you act corruptly by making a graven image for yourselves, in the form of any figure, the likeness of male or female."

In the New Testament, the concept of "Son" is expanded far beyond a male descendant. The Son is identified with the Word or Reason that was with God and yet also was God (John 1:1), the underlying principle by which the universe is held together (Colossians 1:17).

Scientific study of the human brain can inspire awe, as illustrated by the words of renown neuroscientist V. S. Ramachandran, "How can a three-pound mass of jelly that you can hold in your palm imagine angels, contemplate the meaning of infinity, and even question its own place in the cosmos?"[5] For many people, using their brains for these purposes triggers an even greater feeling of awe for a loving God who is behind and beyond all things.

For most people, the human brain is something they have never seen or touched. Their knowledge of the brain is provided in part by images that are incomplete. Likewise, God is something that cannot be seen or touched and can only be understood using mental images that are similarly imperfect. Commitment to God should not be rejected as irrational simply because the mental images it adopts can appear childish or unscientific, any more than doctors should be considered irrational because they rely on CT scans which incorrectly show the brain's grey matter as white and the white matter as grey.

If looking inside the human body reminds us that we are not so different from animals and undermines our self-image as rational beings, perhaps it is right that we should feel uncomfortable. After all, various scanning techniques have contributed to the current biological understanding of how we use our brains for reasoning. And we would share our discomfort with at least one great scientist: Charles Darwin. On 3rd July 1881, he wrote in a letter to philosopher William Graham, "But then with me the horrid doubt always arises whether the convictions of man's mind, which has been developed from the mind of the lower animals, are of any value or at all trustworthy."[6] Today, we have scientific evidence to show that Darwin's misgivings were entirely justified.

5. Ramachandran, *Tell-Tale Brain*, 4.
6. Darwin, "To William Graham 3 July 1881."

Poor Reasoning Can Be Good for Survival

The traditional understanding has been that reason enables us to critically examine our beliefs and make them more reliable by rejecting notions that are incorrect. But, according to a recent review of research in this field conducted by cognitive scientists Hugo Mercier and Dan Sperber, science shows that humans are not particularly good at using reason for decision-making.[7] Human reasoning is typically lazy and can lead to distorted or erroneous beliefs while making little effort to control or check for these shortcomings. Instead of pointing towards better judgments, reasoning usually draws us to decisions that are easier to justify. We tend to search for arguments that support a given conclusion and, all other things being equal, we favor conclusions for which arguments can be found easily.

Humans are also prone to look for arguments that justify their beliefs or actions. Interpreting new evidence as confirmation of one's existing beliefs is a common and strong bias in reasoning, particularly if reasoning alone when there may be nothing to suppress this tendency. Too much reasoning can create undue self-confidence, allowing us to keep unsound or polarized beliefs and create excuses for defying our own moral intuitions.

The classical view that reasoning enhances decision-making is so deep-seated within popular thought that new perspectives can at first seem strange or hard to understand. And this is very much the case for the new scientific understanding of human reason that Mercier and Sperber have proposed. They argue that the classical view of reason does not match the scientific data. The evidence suggests that reason evolved not because it helps individuals to make better beliefs, but because it strengthens social and cognitive interactions. Humans use reason for persuasion by signaling that a communication contains reliable, trustworthy information, rather than dangerous misinformation. By using reason to evaluate the soundness of the arguments offered, the listener gains useful information that he might otherwise distrust. The use of reason by both the speaker and the listener has enhanced the exchange of information between them, to the benefit of each. With this interpretation, those traits that look like defective reasoning from a classical perspective become understandable as tools for improving communication. Poor reasoning can be good for survival.

These findings pose significant challenges to those who claim to use science to defend their lack of belief in God. The science that underpins this

---

7. Mercier and Sperber, *Enigma of Reason*.

worldview suggests that they may have adopted their belief not because it is true, but because it is easier to find arguments to support it. Atheists are by no means immune to this tendency. We have already seen in previous chapters how some people who use science to support their position of unbelief fail to subject their own arguments to rigorous scientific analysis. For example, the claim that scientific knowledge causes people to reject belief in God does not stand up to scrutiny when assessed using established scientific methods for confirming a causal relationship. In moments of honesty, some atheists may even own up to their bias, one famous example being Aldous Huxley, who said:

> I had motives for not wanting the world to have meaning; consequently I assumed that it had none, and was able without any difficulty to find satisfying reasons for this assumption . . . For myself, as no doubt, for most of my contemporaries, the philosophy of meaninglessness was essentially an instrument of liberation. The liberation we desired was simultaneous liberation from a certain political and economic system, and liberation from a certain system of morality.[8]

Some may argue that, regardless of any personal motives for believing only in natural properties and causes, objective evidence of the truth of this worldview can be drawn from its track record of success as demonstrated by the application of this belief system within science. Science would not have been so effective unless its representation of the world were accurate. But this argument is itself an example of human reasoning which science suggests is orientated towards persuasion rather than truth. If better decision-making was not the driving force for the evolution of reason, why should reason be an effective way to disprove the existence of God?

Recognizing connections between objects and events in our immediate surroundings clearly promotes survival. We infer the possibility of a predator from movement in the grass, the risk of falling from being too close to the edge of a high cliff. But these mental processes could be subconscious, as is the case for many animals. However, the ability to communicate these associations is also advantageous. We can point out useful connections to others as a means to increase the likelihood of their acceptance and we can evaluate the connections others give to us. The cost of the additional mental processing involved in reasoning in this way is offset by the survival benefit it creates for the group of which I am a member.

8. Huxley, *Ends and Means*, 273.

But what if someone were to spot a connection between falling off a cliff and the movement of the Moon across the sky? Can we assume that mental processes selected for survival and reproductive success would provide reliable insights of this sort? A detailed understanding of planetary motion would seem to have little value for survival. And yet this is exactly what Isaac Newton did. In fact, humans have achieved several great insights of no immediate practical value and with no possibility of being checked against ordinary experience. It seems questionable that a process of human reasoning which favors argumentation over truth could produce knowledge of this kind. If only natural properties and causes exist, it seems that science as we know it would be impossible. As theoretical physicist and theologian John Polkinghorne put it:

> If one could not figure out that it is a bad idea to step off the top of a high cliff, one might not be around for very long. But our ancestors' need for this prudential knowledge does not explain how someone like Isaac Newton could come along and, in an astonishing creative leap of the human imagination, see that the same force that made the high cliff dangerous was also the force holding the Moon in its orbit round the Earth, and the Earth in its orbit round the Sun, discover the mathematically beautiful law of universal inverse square gravity, and so be able to explain the behavior of the whole solar system . . . Something is going on here which totally transcends the mundane necessities of successful survival, or that could be considered with any degree of plausibility as simply being a spin-off from such necessities.[9]

Reasoning with God

So we have a problem. A perspective that allows for only natural properties and causes suggests that human reasoning did not evolve to establish truth but for persuasion, and yet there is evidence that reasoning can achieve so much more. Perhaps, like the fine-tuning of the universe, this is just another happy coincidence. Alternatively, the origin of reason could lie beyond nature. This possibility would not only fit the scientific data and but also explain why humans can reason about phenomena that are of no value for survival. And it is a proposition we can (or even should) consider if we reinterpret the data reviewed by Mercier and Sperber without the "No God" simplifying

9. Polkinghorne, "Where Is Natural Theology Today?," 172.

assumption. As discussed in chapter 1, testing underlying assumptions in this way should be part of a rigorous evaluation of evidence. Furthermore, seeking explanations that integrate different kinds of evidence is fundamental to the judicious use of evidence. Combining science and faith in this way can give us a deeper understanding of human reason.

For a large number of people, the fact that we encounter a world made up of regularities that are understandable through the use of reason is dependent upon a reality which is more than space–time, matter, and energy. This reality is experienced as a Person and is called God. If reason is primarily a communication tool as science tells us it is, we might expect the source of reason to have the qualities of a person. Rather than emerging from natural processes, reason was present in the mind of God before the existence of the universe, and the rationality of the natural world is a reflection of the character of its creator. Perhaps, then, the function of reason is not simply to strengthen social and cognitive interactions between humans, but also to improve communication between humans and God.

Contrary to simplistic views which consider religious belief to be the opposite of reason, for most people of faith, reason is essential to their commitment to God, and this includes reasoning with God. The idea that reason can be part of a relationship with God is not new. There are plenty of examples of reasoning with God in the Old Testament (such as Genesis 18:23–33, Jonah 4, Isaiah 1:18). We have seen that, in an interpersonal setting, reasoning can signal that a communication contains reliable, trustworthy information rather than potentially dangerous misinformation. When speaking to God, people of faith can use reason to show God that their prayers and their worship are genuine.

When listening to God, the use of reason would not be to prove that his communications are reliable; to be misleading would be against the divine nature. On the other hand, if God provides reasons to accept the information he offers, by evaluating these reasons we can recognize the truthfulness of the knowledge presented and distinguish it from other potentially misleading sources, such as our own minds. By reasoning with God, humans may receive knowledge unconnected with the sorts of things that would be advantageous for their survival and reproduction.

But this is not to say that only people who believe in God can reason in this way. When someone uses reason to gain genuine insights about matters unconnected to the concerns of everyday life, they are in effect engaging with something beyond nature, whether they recognize this as reasoning with God or not. In the words of C. S. Lewis, "the Human mind in the act of knowing is illuminated by the Divine reason."[10] It is this perspective that underpins the use of reason within this book.

Albert Einstein wrote, "Science without religion is lame."[11] The same can be said for all disciplines that depend heavily on accurate reasoning. If only natural properties and causes exist, we are simply highly evolved animals and human reasoning is reduced to a communication aid for passing on basic knowledge conducive to survival and reproduction. Deeper insights require the enlightening rays of God's reason. Perhaps those who are tempted to say, "I do not go to church because I believe in reason and science," should think again.

10. Lewis, *Miracles*, 34.

11. Einstein, *Ideas and Opinions*, 46.

8

The Case for Worship

THE FIRST STEP IN the process of medical diagnosis is usually to take the patient's history. After introducing themselves, the doctor will ask the patient to give an account of their current illness, along with other information such as past illnesses and allergies. Even when listening to the patient's history, the doctor will form an idea about which disease would most likely explain the patient's symptoms. The doctor will ask specific questions to test this hypothesis. On hearing the answers, the doctor will update their assessment of the probability that the patient has the disease in question. Further updating occurs during the clinical examination, including what is heard through the stethoscope. If additional diagnostic tests, such as blood samples, X-rays, and scans, are required, the probability of the presumed diagnosis continues to change as the results become available.

Medical diagnosis is not a haphazard process, but is scientific. This method for updating the probability for a hypothesis as more evidence or information becomes available is known as Bayesian inference and follows the principles of a statistical method first described by the English clergyman Reverend Thomas Bayes (1702–1761). Today, Bayes' theorem is used widely throughout science and is an example of an important contribution to science made by a person of faith.

Belief as a Bayesian Process

It is possible to conceive of belief as being an all-or-nothing process. You either believe something or you don't. But based on recent theories in the field of neuropsychology, the way people form and evaluate beliefs can be more accurately described using Bayes theorem. These approaches to belief allow for varying degrees of confidence in an idea or a proposition that are broadly similar to the thought processes used by doctors to reach a diagnosis, as described earlier.

Imagine you are a juror in a court hearing of someone accused of murder. You have two competing hypotheses: A—the defendant is guilty, or B—the defendant is not guilty. Your confidence in each of these hypotheses can be represented as a probability value which reflects the likelihood of each proposition being true. Maybe at first you think each hypothesis has a 50:50 chance of being true, but these probability values change as you hear the evidence presented by the lawyers for the prosecution and defense. At some point, you may decide to commit to one or other of the hypotheses and say either, "I believe the defendant is guilty," or, "I believe the defendant is not guilty." In a murder case, this will most likely happen when the probability value exceeds a certain threshold. In other circumstances, someone may commit to a belief when the probability for one hypothesis is simply greater than a competing proposition.

The Value of Information

With advances in medical technology, there is an ever-increasing number of diagnostic tests that can contribute to diagnosis in different ways. None is 100 percent accurate, but it is impracticable for clinicians to request more and more tests in order to get as much information as possible before deciding on the best treatment. Inevitably, clinical decisions are usually made with less-than-perfect information. But there is a scientific way to decide whether it is worth looking for more clinical data. It is possible to estimate the benefits of having perfect information and comparing them to the disadvantages (if any) involved in getting that information. If the disadvantages are greater than the benefits, there is no point asking for more information.

For example, imagine you are a doctor who is looking after a patient with a cough and a fever. The chest X-ray you have arranged for the patient suggests pneumonia. Chest X-rays are effective at diagnosing pneumonia but not perfect. You can now choose to prescribe antibiotics on the basis of the chest X-ray or do more tests to improve your diagnostic confidence. But if there were no more tests available, you would have to decide based on the chest X-ray alone, and the table below summarizes your options. If you prescribe antibiotics and the patient does have pneumonia, their condition improves, but if there is no pneumonia, the patient will receive antibiotics unnecessarily. On the other hand, if you were to offer no treatment and the patient has pneumonia, they will most likely get worse, but if they there is no pneumonia, you will have avoided giving unnecessary antibiotics.

Decision	Pneumonia present	No pneumonia
Prescribe antibiotics	Condition improves	Unnecessary antibiotics
No treatment	Condition worsens	No treatment necessary

Table 1: Decision matrix for a patient with a cough and fever and a chest X-ray suggesting pneumonia

If you had perfect information, you would give antibiotics only if they were really needed. By comparing the decision made with perfect information against the best decision that could be made based on the chest X-ray, you can work out the expected value of perfect information (EVPI). In this case, the EVPI reflects the benefit of avoiding unnecessary antibiotics in the event that the patient turns out *not* to have pneumonia. (Normally, the EVPI would be expressed numerically in monetary terms, but for simplicity, a qualitative approach is used here.) Notice that the EVPI is determined by what might happen if there is no pneumonia.

Now that we have defined what is at stake in our decision-making, we can consider whether getting more information is worthwhile. A CT scan of the lungs would get us closer to perfect information, but even CT is not 100 percent accurate. Moreover, there are some disadvantages in doing a CT scan. The scan will expose the patient to more radiation and, from the payer's point of view (e.g., a government or insurance company funding healthcare, or an individual paying for their own private medical treatment), CT involves an additional financial cost. These disadvantages could be considered to outweigh the benefit of avoiding unnecessary antibiotics and it may be best to make your decision using the chest X-ray alone—that is, with less-than-perfect information. The CT scan could be held in reserve should the patient not improve.

The Value of Evidence for God

Extraordinary claims require extraordinary evidence. This saying sums up the attitude of many atheists towards the existence of God. But is this position supported by decision science? In principle, the question is similar to the one we considered earlier: does a chest X-ray provide sufficient information to prescribe antibiotics for a presumptive diagnosis of pneumonia? And we can use a similar decision analysis to answer it. Moreover, when we do, we find that there is no point looking for more evidence of God's existence unless correct unbelief (i.e., atheism) is better than believing in God even if he does not exist.

Just as prescribing antibiotics is an appropriate medical response to a diagnosis of pneumonia, worship is an appropriate response to the existence of a creator God who is the source of all goodness and the foundation of reason. Earlier chapters have outlined a number of considerations that can motivate people to worship such a God, and these can be summed up as follows:

- The way science allows for only natural properties and causes is a simplifying assumption. Questioning assumptions is part of the scientific process. It is therefore valid to re-evaluate scientific data from a perspective that allows for the existence of a reality beyond the natural world.

- An awareness of a reality (called God) that is more than the natural world of space–time, matter, and energy, one that also created, sustains, and interacts with the natural world, is an experience that is sufficiently common to be worthy of inclusion in serious theorizing.

- Rather than discounting such experiences entirely and so risk losing unique insights about the cosmos and human life, they can be evaluated within a hierarchy of evidence (illustrated by a pyramid).

- Because these experiences cannot be verified independently, they carry less weight than experimental data that can be independently verified (i.e., scientific data). However, being based on actual data, they lie above expert opinion and evidence from first principles alone.

- The weight of these experiences as evidence for God is increased by being part of a network of related experiences and theories, and by the impact they have on the behavior of the lives of the individuals undergoing the experience and the communities in which they live.

- The weight of evidence is also stronger when these experiences can be shown to be consistent with experimental data that can be independently verified. In fact, there are circumstances when scientific data fits better with the experience of God than with philosophical concepts based on first principles (e.g., fine-tuning, the moral sense, and reason).

Regardless of how compelling these arguments might be, being primarily based on lived experiences that cannot be obtained at will, they provide less-than-perfect information about the existence of God. But are they sufficient to support a decision to worship God despite uncertainty? The table below summarizes the options concerning worshipping God, analogous to the decision regarding antibiotic treatment for a presumptive diagnosis of pneumonia as described above. If you worship God and he does exist, you gain the benefits of correct belief, but if he does not exist, your worship will have been unnecessary. On the other hand, if you do not worship God and he does exist, you will suffer the detrimental effects of unbelief (if any), but if there is no God, you will have avoided worshipping needlessly. I have deliberately left vague the benefits gained from worshipping God if he exists, as well as the corresponding detrimental effects of unbelief.

Notice that we are not using this decision matrix to argue that it is rational to believe in God, but for the more modest objective of determining whether it is worthwhile seeking more information before choosing to worship as part of a commitment to God. Just as for the case of pneumonia, we can do this by estimating the Expected Value of Perfect Information (EVPI) for God's existence, and the EVPI is primarily determined by what might happen if there is no God. The exact size of the benefits gained from worshipping God if he exists is therefore unimportant because it does not affect the EVPI. For commitment to God to be the better decision, these benefits simply need to be very large in comparison to the probability of gaining them, and this is the case not just for Christianity but for all major faith traditions.

Decision	God exists	There is no God
Worship God	Benefits of appropriate worship	Unnecessary worship
Do not worship God	Detrimental effects of no worship	No worship necessary

Table 2: Decision matrix for worshipping God[1]

1. Some readers will notice that this decision matrix is very similar to Pascal's wager. But there are important differences. Pascal used his wager to illustrate that belief in God is rational, not to determine the value of information about God's existence. Furthermore, by not specifying an infinite benefit from correct belief in God, an important limitation of Pascal's wager is avoided. The appreciation of an infinite gain may be beyond our conceptual abilities and the use of infinity can distort any decisions that are based on Pascal's wager, not only conceptually but also mathematically.

Perfect information about God's existence would indeed be extraordinary evidence to support the extraordinary claims of religious belief. But the decision science outlined above shows that this perfect information would only have value if believing that God does not exist were more favorable than believing in God even if he does not exist. If it were the other way around, and believing in God even if he doesn't exist is equal to or better than atheism, then then the EVPI will be zero or less. And if perfect information has no value, any additional evidence for God would also be worthless.

In one episode from C. S. Lewis' *The Chronicles of Narnia*, Puddleglum is challenging the Queen of Underland who has been trying to convince him, Eustace, and Jill that Narnia does not exist.

> Suppose we have only dreamed, or made up, all those things— trees and grass and sun and moon and stars and Aslan himself. Suppose we have. Then all I can say is that, in that case, the made-up things seem a good deal more important than the real ones. Suppose this black pit of a kingdom of yours is the only world. Well, it strikes me as a pretty poor one. And that's a funny thing, when you come to think of it. We're just babies making up a game, if you're right. But four babies playing a game can make a play-world which licks your real world hollow. That's why I'm going to stand by the play world. I'm on Aslan's side even if there isn't any Aslan to lead it. I'm going to live as like a Narnian as I can even if there isn't any Narnia.[2]

In this series of books, Narnia corresponds to the life of faith, while Aslan represents God made known in Jesus Christ. The passage suggests that it is better to believe in God even if it is not true. And if Puddleglum is right, there would be no point asking for more evidence of God's existence.

Of course, many atheists would disagree with Puddleglum. They consider that belief in God has negative effects, both on the individual and on society. But does the evidence support this position? Earlier chapters have not only shown this assertion to be incorrect, but also highlighted some of the benefits of belief in God. Although religion is vulnerable to being hijacked by those with violent intentions, established scientific criteria fail to demonstrate that religious faith causes violence. Those who claim otherwise need to explain why this scientific methodology should not apply in this case. We have also seen that belief in God does not give license to others to hold unsubstantiated beliefs that may be harmful. Although

---

2. Lewis, *Silver Chair*, 145.

approaching religion as a means to an end, or as a set of unquestionable beliefs that are handed down from above, can be associated with intolerance, belief in God does not have to be approached in those ways. This effect is not found when faith is seen as a quest for knowledge.

Belief in God has inspired many things that have enriched civilization, including works of art and music. The concept of universal human rights has its origins in Christianity. Even modern science emerged in a Christian context and many of its basic assumptions have their origins in Christian thinking (as discussed earlier). Benefits to the lives of individuals committed to God can be seen to follow from participation in public worship and other practices that aim to facilitate interactions with the reality of God. As will be discussed in more detail later, regular attendance at public expressions of worship is associated with fewer health problems and a longer life span, not only in comparison to people who are socially isolated but also relative to those who are supported by secular social networks. Contemplative practices, such as focused prayer and meditation, reduce stress which, if chronic, increases susceptibility to a wide range of illnesses. An attitude of mind inspired by religious faith can also activate health-enhancing mind–body interactions that are now regarded to underlie the placebo effect (see also chapter 3).

It is common for skeptics to base their unbelief on a lack of proof for God's existence. When asking for more evidence, some may think they are being scientific. But how often do they use decision science to determine the value of the information they are asking for? Starting from a neutral position where there is no prejudgment as to which outcome is better if God doesn't exist, even perfect information for God's existence would be of no value because the EVPI would be zero. Therefore, before asking for more evidence of God's existence, there is an onus on skeptics to demonstrate that correct unbelief is better than worshipping God even if he doesn't exist, which may be difficult or impossible, given the contrary evidence outlined above.

—— Part Two ——

Worship in Action

9

Healing and a God Who Acts

In June 1963, a young man named Vittorio Micheli went to the Sanctuary of Our Lady of Lourdes, France, hoping to be cured. He had first sought medical help in April 1962, five months after enlisting in the Italian Army. Aged twenty-two, he had been suffering with increasing pain in his left buttock for a few weeks and was now having difficulty walking. The examining doctor detected an ill-defined mass in the patient's left pelvic region, along with shortening of his left leg. An X-ray showed destruction of the socket of the left hip joint and the adjacent bone. Microscopic examination of a sample of tissue from the affected region revealed a malignant tumor known as a sarcoma.

A series of X-rays performed over the next seven months showed progressive worsening of the bone destruction. At no time did Micheli receive anti-cancer treatment. At one point, his doctors considered giving him radiation treatment but decided against it because they thought it would be unlikely to help. He was given painkilling medication, and a plaster cast extending from his hip to his foot was applied to assist with pain relief.

On arrival at Lourdes in June the following year, Micheli was immersed in the bath water with his leg cast still on. As soon as he was in the water, he said he felt hungry. From then on, he no longer needed painkillers and was able to walk with the aid of crutches. In February 1964, when the cast was finally removed, Micheli could walk without pain, suffering only a slight limp. X-rays taken between 1964 and 1971 show that the previously destroyed areas of bone had regrown. Micheli went on to help the sick at Lourdes for several decades.[1]

---

1. Neilan, "Miraculous Cure."

X-rays as Evidence

A little more than a year after Roentgen's discovery, X-ray images were used for the first time as evidence within a court of law.[2] The patient, James Smith, had been injured in a fall from a ladder while trimming some trees. Sometime later, he consulted a distinguished surgeon, who did not splint the thigh but advised various exercises as though the injury were just a severe bruise. X-ray images of the hip showed an abnormal position of the head of the thigh bone in relation to the shaft and were therefore submitted as evidence that the bone had in fact been fractured. The defense lawyers objected on grounds that the images could not be proven to be an accurate portrayal of an object unseen by the human eye, but the presiding judge ruled that the radiographs could be accepted as secondary evidence.

The use of X-ray images for forensic purposes is now well established, and Micheli's X-ray images were included when his case was investigated by the Lourdes Medical Bureau and subsequently recognized as miraculous by the church. But can X-rays confidently confirm that a miracle has happened? If so, would that persuade people to believe in the existence of God? Philosopher Matthew S. McCormick seems to think so. In *Atheism and the Case Against Christ*, he suggests that the ability of divine intervention to encourage belief in God might be improved if X-ray evidence were to be provided for alleged miraculous healings.[3] Perhaps he was unaware that X-rays had been a part of the evaluation of Micheli's extraordinary healing.

Divine Action and the Laws of Nature

Like many skeptics, McCormick repeats the argument against miracles proposed by Scottish philosopher David Hume (1711–1776). Atheist writer Christopher Hitchens does the same. In his book *God is Not Great*, Hitchens considers Hume to have written "the last word on the subject." Hume defined a miracle as a violation of a law of nature, stating, "No testimony is sufficient to establish a miracle, unless the testimony be of such a kind, that its falsehood would be more miraculous than the fact which it endeavors to establish." According to Hume, no testimony can be

---

2. Withers, "Story of the First Roentgen Evidence."
3. McCormick, "Why Are All of the Gods Hiding?," 390.

adequate to establish a miracle. It is always more likely that the evidence in favor of a miracle will be false.[4]

Written nearly 150 years before the discovery of X-rays, Hume's argument could not have taken into account the potential for X-rays or other medical tests to be included as evidence for divine action. But if Hume were alive today, perhaps he would consider it to be more miraculous for an X-ray to give false information than for a divine healing to actually occur. It is well recognized that flaws in X-ray image quality can cause imaging errors. I recall a patient who came for a scan to investigate what was thought to be destruction of an arm bone on an earlier X-ray. When the follow-up scan showed normal bone, we concluded that the appearance on the initial X-ray was actually an imaging defect. At no point did we consider the possibility of a miracle.

In the 1960s, when Micheli would have had his investigations, conventional X-ray film would have been used rather than the digital X-ray equipment used today. This film is sensitive not only to X-rays but also to pressure. If stored incorrectly, a weight of some kind pressing on part of a film could create an area that would appear over-exposed once the X-ray had been taken. If this happened to coincide with the position of a patient's hip, the bone in this area could appear to have been destroyed. X-ray evidence would seem to be no less vulnerable to Hume's argument. Despite McCormick's assertion, it seems that someone who holds to Hume's view of miracles is even unlikely to consider X-ray evidence as sufficient confirmation of divine healing.

There is another inconsistency in suggesting that X-ray images could be used to confirm a violation of the laws of nature. How can X-ray images be considered reliable if there is a possibility that the natural laws involved in the X-ray imaging process are themselves open to interference? Bones are visible on X-rays because the calcium within the bones blocks the passage of X-rays more than the water and fat that make up the surrounding soft tissues. Rather than a miraculous cure, there is always the possibility that the laws of nature could be broken such that the ability of soft tissue to block X-rays was changed to give the appearance of restored bone on the resulting image.

---

4. Cited in Hitchens, *God Is Not Great*. 141.

God's Cooperation with Nature

In the early 1960s, regrowth of bone destroyed by cancer would have seemed to be an astounding breach of normal biological processes. But nearly sixty years have passed since then, and in that time there have been significant improvements in both medical imaging and cancer treatment. Today, the medical literature includes several reports of patients with bones that have regrown after being destroyed by cancer. In one case, the affected bone was in a similar part of the body as Vittorio Micheli.[5] I have seen two such cases myself and, surprisingly, the restored bone looks almost perfect. But, unlike Micheli, these patients had received cancer therapy, sometimes combined with drugs that inhibit the resorption of bone. Based on these cases, we now know that biological processes exist which enable bones to regrow even when destroyed by cancer.

How do these advances in medical science alter our understanding of Vittorio Micheli's apparent cure? By no means do they exclude the possibility of divine healing (for those who are open to that prospect). Remember, Micheli had received no anti-cancer treatment. Even today, spontaneous resolution of a malignant sarcoma would be considered astonishing. But the fact that destroyed bone can regrow with treatment does say something about how God might act. It seems that medical science has managed to reproduce something that God had achieved decades before. Rather than violating natural processes altogether, God appears to heal by using biological mechanisms that are already in place.

The idea that God acts by cooperating with nature predates Hume's position on miracles by many centuries. The early Christian theologian and philosopher, Augustine of Hippo (AD 354–430), held that a miracle is not against nature but contrary only to what is known of nature. This view fits perfectly with Micheli's case. The ability for bone to regrow after being destroyed by cancer was unknown in 1963 when Micheli went to Lourdes, but has since become recognized by medical science. And the same is likely to apply to other miracles that appear to be contrary to scientific laws today.

The notion that God would break the laws of nature creates other problems. If violating the character of the things God has created were not contrary to his divine nature, we would need to ask why he doesn't break the laws of nature more often—for example, to avert natural disasters and

---

5. Kishimoto et al., "Reossification of Osteolytic Metastases."

other causes of suffering. And why would he need to break his own laws if he had made them perfectly in the first place?

Within the network of experiences and theories that constitute Christian thinking, we find the concept that the actions of Jesus of Nazareth show the character of God, and these actions support the view that God acts through cooperation with nature. The Gospel account of Matthew describes the temptation of Jesus in the wilderness (Matthew 4:3). Although hungry after fasting for forty days and nights, Jesus refuses to turn stones into bread. Jesus and God alike respect the inherent character of the things God has created, and stones changing into bread is not something that would happen even with a perfect relationship between God and nature.

As C. S. Lewis points out, divine actions are not arbitrary interruptions of natural processes by God to achieve a particular purpose, but are all connected to the reality of God becoming human.[6] This special act of God which is central to Christianity signifies the beginning of a process that will restore the relationship between God and the world, make good his broken creation, and repair the effects of humankind's rejection of God. All divine actions will therefore reflect this overall plan of God for his creation. Those events that are described as miracles are moments in which we see how nature would behave when a proper relationship between nature and God has been restored.

But what about the Resurrection of Jesus? This event is central to Christianity. As St Paul bluntly put it, "if Christ has not been raised, then our preaching is in vain and your faith is in vain" (1 Corinthians 15:14). Can we expect our understanding of the Resurrection to follow the same course as our understanding of the regrowth of Micheli's pelvic bone? Will there be a time when scientific knowledge of death will mean that even the Resurrection could be understood as God's cooperation with nature?

In his book *2084*, Christian mathematician John Lennox points to writers who have predicted that humans may one day have the knowledge to achieve immortality and even resurrection. He quotes Russian Philosopher Nikolai Fedorov (1829–1903), who wrote that "resurrection will be a task not of miracle but of knowledge and common labor."[7] More recently, Israeli historian Yuval Harari has described human death as a "technical glitch" for which there should be technical solution.[8] Perhaps

---

6. Lewis, *Miracles*, 173.

7. Fedorov, cited in Lennox, *2084*, 87.

8. Harari, *Homo Deus*, 22.

gene-based technologies will allow the biological processes that underlie death to be stopped or reversed. Alternatively, ever-closer connections between humans and technology may eventually enable our minds to be uploaded into a computer. "We don't need to wait for the second coming in order to overcome death," writes Harari.[9]

The regrowth of bone destroyed by cancer that sometimes happens with certain treatments today is very similar to that seen for Micheli after his visit to Lourdes. But the same cannot be said for the defeat of death envisaged by Harari and others. As Lennox makes clear, regardless of its plausibility, their vision is very different from the circumstances of the Resurrection of Jesus. His Resurrection did not just bring about the reversal of death into life, but also a state of having risen from the dead which was not the same as before. Yet this was not some kind of supernatural occurrence in a spiritual realm that people were somehow able to experience. If that were the case, there would be no point asking whether the Resurrection represented God's cooperation with the laws of nature. This was undeniably a physical resurrection, as Jesus himself made clear to his disciples. "See my hands and my feet, that it is I myself; handle me, and see; for a spirit has not flesh and bones as you see that I have" (Luke 24:39). But this was a new mode of existence. Jesus was able to appear and disappear; locked doors were no barrier for him, and on a number of occasions he was not immediately recognizable to those who knew him.

Within the network of interconnected experiences and theories that underlie Christian thinking, the events around the Resurrection of Jesus can be interpreted in the context of the future transformation of the universe, as outlined in chapter 6. The risen state of Jesus gives us a preview of what this new creation will be like. The transformation of our present universe will involve changes to the laws of nature in ways that are hard to anticipate. And we have very little data to go on. There was only a six-week opportunity to observe this foretaste of the new creation, and the only possible relic that is available for scientific analysis today is the Shroud of Turin, believed by some to be the burial cloth of Jesus. Nevertheless, at some point in the future, humankind will be able to experience the new creation and the accompanying changes in the laws of nature. But then, the relationship between humankind and nature will also be renewed, such that there may be no need for a fresh scientific endeavor to work out these new laws. Regardless, it should become possible to determine

9. Harari, *Homo Deus*, 23.

whether the Resurrection of Jesus represents God's cooperation with nature. But if God acts in our current world by cooperating with nature, he is likely to do the same in the new creation.

Evidence for Divine Action

Healing is an important aspect of public worship. It is common for church services to include prayers for the healing of individuals. Sometimes acts of worship dedicated to healing are performed, such as the laying-on of hands, which may also be accompanied by anointing with oil. It is unusual for healings as dramatic as Micheli's to occur during these events, but the possibility that God could at some point heal the individuals concerned is fundamental to these forms of worship. However, the concept of God's interaction with nature is not just relevant to healing. It applies to any experience of God, not only during worship but also at other times. Just as is the case for healing, these experiences will involve God's cooperation with natural processes.

In 2015–2016, British illusionist Derren Brown went on tour with a show entitled "Miracles" in which he simulated faith-healing. He appeared to fix poor eyesight and cure internal aches and pains. Are the events that are believed to be divine healing simply illusions like these? The fact that some faith-healers may be charlatans does not exclude the possibility of genuine divine action. The word "miracle" comes from the Latin word *mirari*, which means "to wonder." God's action should therefore be recognizable from the kind of experience it creates. In chapter 5, we considered an evidence-based approach that uses three criteria to evaluate religious experience, and two of these are applicable here: does the experience form part of a network of interconnected experiences and theories, and are there corresponding lasting effects on the life of the individual and the community in which they live?

We have already seen how some actions are incompatible with the network of experiences and theories that underlie Christian thinking. Turning stones into bread, for example. But the most important evidence for God's interaction with nature will be found in the way the lives of people experiencing the event are transformed. An increase in unconditional love for others is the hallmark of a true encounter with God. This is unlikely to happen after going to an illusionist's show, but can certainly be seen in the dramatic changes in the lives of Jesus's followers after they had witnessed the miracle of the Resurrection. Immediately after Jesus's death, they were timid and afraid. But after encountering the risen Jesus, they became bold and full of joy, proclaiming their experiences even in the face of suffering and torture. In the same way, we can see how Vittorio Micheli was transformed by his healing, choosing to dedicate the rest of his life to helping the sick at Lourdes.

10

Billiards Balls and Bishops

JANE IS HAVING A CT scan of her kidneys, not because she is sick but because she has offered one of her kidneys to her sister Louise who needs a renal transplant because her kidneys are failing. Jane has seen her sister have many different medical tests during her illness, but now it is her turn. At first, she was a little surprised that she had to have so many tests herself; after all, she is perfectly well. But she now understands that it is important to check out her own kidneys thoroughly before donating one of them to Louise. The CT scan today will show up the arteries and veins to her kidneys. Normally there is one artery and one vein supplying each kidney, but sometimes there can be two or even three, which would make the surgery difficult or even impossible. Fortunately, Jane has only one artery and vein on each side and so can donate her kidney to Louise. But research has shown that these and other variations in blood vessel anatomy are becoming more common over time,[1] and this is thought to be an example of human microevolution.

Microevolution refers to evolutionary changes that occur over a short period of time—for example, over a few successive generations.[2] The sections of DNA that make up our genes determine the anatomical structure of our bodies as well as the way our bodies function. Blood vessels develop in the human embryo through a highly organized sequence of events which requires the right genes to be switched on and off in the right place at the right time. Changes in these genes may lead to alterations in the arrangement of blood vessels in our bodies. If we reproduce,

1. Saniotis and Henneberg, "Anatomical Variations and Evolution."
2. Rühli et al., "Evolutionary Medicine."

these changes can be passed on to our children, who may pass them on to their children, and so on.

Evolutionary theory can explain why variations in body structure like these are becoming more common. The chance that the biological changes resulting from alterations in genetic make-up are passed on to the next generation fundamentally depends on the probability that the individual will reproduce, and this probability has increased drastically in recent centuries. Until the mid-nineteenth century, the chance of reaching fifteen years of age was approximately 50 percent. Today, more than 90 percent of newborn children will have an opportunity to take part in the reproduction of the next generation. This decrease in the pressure of natural selection will result in greater variability in human anatomy.

An increasing variability in human anatomy does not prove that humans have evolved from other species. Nevertheless, past evolutionary events can account for present-day conditions of the human body and, given the compelling evidence for evolution by natural selection in general, there is little need to suggest alternative explanations for the development of human beings. But can this scientific account of human development be reconciled with the religious idea that God intentionally created human beings to be creatures who worship?

The previous chapter emphasized that God acts by cooperating with nature rather than by breaking natural laws, in which case it should be possible to propose a mechanism through which God could act within the processes of evolution by natural selection. One potential opening lies in the processes of gene mutation which create the biological variations that are subject to natural selection. Changes that promote survival and/or reproductive success are more likely to be passed on to the next generation. Natural sources of ionizing radiation are believed to be responsible for many of these mutations. A cosmic ray, for example, hits a reproductive cell of an organism and causes a change or mutation in the DNA, which in turn produces a new characteristic within the offspring of the organism. Depending on the conditions of the environment in which the organism is living, the new characteristic may give the organism a survival advantage. Because the organism is more likely to survive, it is more likely to pass that characteristic on to the next generation. If the new characteristic represents a survival disadvantage, the organism is less likely to be able to pass the characteristic to future generations. In this way, the organism may change over time, adapting to its environment as new favorable characteristics are accrued.

The cosmic ray alters DNA indirectly by displacing an electron (known as a secondary electron) which moves around within the tissues of the organism, causing damage to DNA and other molecules on account of its negative charge. The motion of the secondary electron is rather like a billiard ball bouncing off the sides of the billiard table several times. The electron changes direction and loses energy each time it interacts with an atom within the tissue. If any of these interactions are with DNA, a mutation may be induced within the DNA. The precise location of the damage within the DNA molecule will determine the properties of the new characteristic induced in the gene line.

Secondary electrons and billiard balls both follow the mathematical principles of chaos theory. Chaos theory relates to systems that can behave unpredictably and are classically very sensitive to initial conditions. This is the idea that a movement of air created by a butterfly's wings in the Amazon Rainforest can result in a hurricane in Florida. In fact, the weather is a good example of a chaotic system, which is why the weather cannot be reliably predicted beyond a few days. It is not possible to determine the initial weather conditions with sufficient precision to make reliable longer-term predictions.

In the case of billiard balls, chaotic behavior can be demonstrated using a computer model known as mathematical billiards. The system is a representation of normal billiards but with no friction and no pockets. The balls bounce around following the same rules as real billiard balls, only they keep going forever. They travel in straight lines at a constant speed, and when they bounce off the sides of the table, they are reflected back, just like a real ball.

Consider a mathematical billiard ball that starts at the middle point of one side of a rectangular table and its direction of travel forms a perfect right angle with the table side. The ball will strike the middle of the opposite wall and bounce backwards and forwards between these points (figure 3A). If the billiard ball starts at the same point but sets off towards the mid-point of one side of the table, it will hit the mid-point of that side, then the mid-point of the far side, followed by the mid-point of the other side before returning to its starting position (figure 3B).

But if we change the direction of travel very slightly from either of the above scenarios, the motion of the ball becomes erratic, never retracing its steps (figure 3C). And if you change the starting position of direction of travel ever so slightly, after a few bounces, the trajectory of the mathematical billiard ball will be different again.

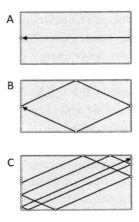

Figure 3. Mathematical Billiards

Let us now look at a worship-related example that demonstrates chaos theory in more detail. (Once, when I presented this model to a church audience, someone thought I was making a serious proposal. Please be assured that this is meant to be tongue in cheek.)

The model is as follows:

The percentage of parishioners attending church next week is determined by three things:

- the "priest's missional factor" *multiplied by*
- the percentage of parishioners attending last week, *multiplied by*
- the percentage of parishioners who did not attend last week.

The "priest's missional factor" or PMR, encapsulates the energy and enthusiasm with which he or she spreads the Christian faith. The graphs below (figure 4) show how attendance (y axis) develops over time (x axis) as we alter the PMR. When the PMR is low, the proportion of parishioners attending church falls over time, and by about week ten, hardly anybody is coming to church. If we increase the PMR a little, attendance rises to about

35 percent and then remains stable. For slightly higher values of PMR, attendance increases to a higher plateau of about 50 percent.

So far so good. But if we increase PMR even more, interesting things start to happen. With a value of 3.0, attendance rises and then oscillates between two values. This pattern corresponds to the mathematical billiard ball bouncing back and forth across the table. Increase the PMR again and we see an even more complex pattern where attendance oscillates between two pairs of values, equivalent to the mathematical billiard ball bouncing off the four sides of the table. But when the PMR reaches 3.7, attendance begins to become completely erratic. It is under these circumstances that the system becomes sensitive to initial conditions.

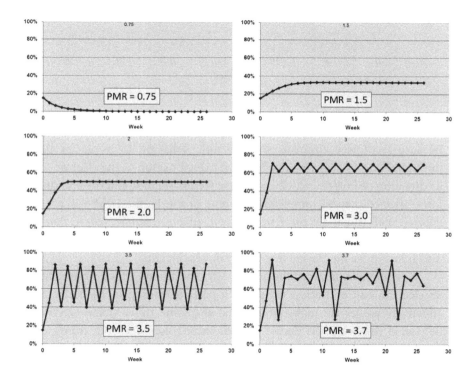

Figure 4

The next graph below (figure 5) shows what happens if we keep the PMR at 3.7 but change the initial number of parishioners attending church (week 0) by a small amount, say 1 percent. We see that for a few weeks, the attendance records track quite closely, but after about five weeks there is a very clear separation of the two curves. At week fourteen, the approximately 75 percent attendance seen with the first starting value has fallen to about 25 percent. So, if week fourteen happens to be when the bishop is visiting, you might wish the extra parishioners hadn't attended at week o!

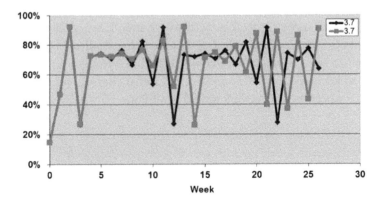

Figure 5

Because secondary electrons show chaotic behavior, their precise path through tissues is also sensitive to the starting position of the electron and its direction of movement. Change these factors slightly, and the section of DNA affected may be completely different, or maybe the DNA will not be affected at all. But as discussed in chapter 4, quantum physics tells us that we can never determine the position and direction of an electron with certainty. This is known as the Heisenberg uncertainty principle.

Chapter 4 considered the double-slit experiment, which showed how an electron can be both a wave and a particle. Strangely, each electron effectively passes through both slits at the same time. When electrons behave in this way, it is known as "quantum coherence." But things can get weirder than that. If you put a detector next to the slits to see which one the electron passes through, the coherence is lost. The wave function collapses and the electrons behave as particles. If you leave the detector there but switch it off, the electrons act as waves again. The observer can choose how the electrons behave. It seems the quantum world is not only full of uncertainty but can also be influenced by the mind.

The BBC book, *The Eight Doctors*, written by Terrance Dicks, describes an occasion when the fifth Dr Who and his companions are attacked by a

Raston Warrior Robot. Through the mysteries of time travel, they are joined by a future regeneration of Dr Who, the eighth Doctor. The two Doctors approach the robot at the same pace, making sure that they both are equidistant from it. Here is how the book describes what happened next:

> Astonishingly, the robot did not attack either of them. It swung from one to the other as if about to fire, but never did. As the Doctors approached nearer and nearer, the robot froze into immobility. Then, clasping its hands to its head in a curiously human gesture, it toppled over, rolling down the hillock to land at the Doctors' feet.[3]

This story is based on a paradox known as Buridan's ass. It refers to a hypothetical situation where a hungry donkey is placed at equal distances from two piles of hay that are identical in size. Unable to decide which pile to go for, the donkey dies of starvation. Philosopher Nancey Murphy has proposed that electrons can be considered as Buridan's asses in that they remain in a state of quantum coherence as a wave of probability unless something causes the wave to collapse.[4] We have seen from the double-slit experiment how the mind can cause the wave to collapse simply by observing the electrons' behavior. Murphy suggests that God can cause the wave to collapse in a similar way, determining the exact position of the electron as the quantum coherence is lost, but without violating the laws of nature.

When quantum coherence is linked to a chaotic system, there will be opportunities for tiny changes at the quantum level to result in larger effects downstream. If the divine mind can determine the position of an electron, this tiny change could in principle be amplified within a chaotic system. And with perfect knowledge of the starting conditions, the exact character of the knock-on effects will be predictable by God.

How might this relate to the processes of evolution? You will remember that an electron behaves as a wave until its position is measured, at which moment the wave function is said to collapse and the electron then behaves as a particle. When displaced by a cosmic ray, the secondary electron will initially behave like a wave. The wave collapses at a given point, after which the movement of the electron becomes like the billiard ball. Just like the mathematical billiard ball (and the church congregation), the path of the secondary electron is sensitive to initial conditions. If you change very slightly the point at which the electron's wave function collapses, the path

3. Dicks, *Eight Doctors*, 171–72.
4. Murphy, "Divine Action in the Natural Order."

of the electron is completely different, interacting with the DNA at a different position or maybe not at all, which in turn would lead to different new characteristics in the next generation. So by changing the point at which the electron changes from a wave to a particle, it is theoretically possible to change where a mutation occurs in DNA. As described earlier, if the mind of God can influence when the wave function of an electron collapses, God could select from a range of possible gene mutations.

In this chapter, we have been looking at the behavior of electrons. There is an old joke about a different elementary particle known as the Higgs boson. The boson decides to go to church and meets the priest at the door. The priest says, "We don't often see your kind in church," to which the boson replies, "Well, you can't have mass without me."

The Higgs boson is an elementary particle that gives material things the property of mass. Existence of the Higgs boson was inferred from theoretical physics sometime before it could be detected physically. The inability to detect the boson was owing to the fact that it interacts only weakly with other particles.

There is an analogy here with the demonstration of divine action. If God does not break the laws of nature, divine action will be hard, if not impossible, to detect by scientific observation. Yet many people regard certain events described in the Bible or experienced by individuals as being due to a God who acts. Indeed, this conception of God is an essential part of the network of experiences and theories that comprise Christian thinking. But as emphasized in the evidence pyramid described in chapter 6, more weight can be given to experiential evidence of this kind (level 3) when it is shown to be compatible rather than inconsistent with scientific data (level 1 evidence). It is therefore useful to identify science-based mechanisms through which God could interact with things within nature, not only inanimate objects such as DNA but also the minds of those who claim to experience God.

By providing a non-religious explanation for apparent design within nature, renowned atheist Richard Dawkins has said that Darwin's theory of natural selection made it possible for him to be an intellectually fulfilled atheist. By pointing to a degree of openness within nature that can allow for the possibility of God acting within creation by cooperating with the laws of nature, quantum mechanics and chaos theory make it possible to be an intellectually fulfilled theist.

— 11 —

A Still, Small Voice

IT STARTS WHEN HE senses a bright, beautiful, and expanding light appearing over his left shoulder. He feels calm and at peace. The bright light forms a tunnel, at the end of which there is an angelic figure who calls him by his name and tells him, "It is not your time." The episode finishes with a bolt of light being thrown at his chest which leaves him with a sensation of unconditional love.

The passage above describes the experience of a seventy-seven-year-old retired physician during epileptic seizures that he suffered intermittently following a head injury thirty years previously. A magnetic resonance scan of his brain had confirmed damage to the temporal lobe on the right side. His case was reported in the scientific literature in 2011 by Enrique Carrazana and Jocelyn Cheng, who highlighted the similarities between the patient's history and the well-known mystical experiences of St Teresa of Ávila, a sixteenth-century Spanish Carmelite nun.[1] An account of the saint's most famous experience was included in Pope Gregory XV's bull of her canonization and has provided inspiration for several works of art, perhaps most notably Gian Lorenzo Bernini's sculpture, "The Ecstasy of Saint Teresa," located at the Cornaro Chapel in Santa Maria della Vittoria, Rome.

An association between epilepsy and religious features is well recognized, but does this connection indicate that spiritual experiences are simply abnormalities of brain function? This notion is not a new one. Karl Marx, Sigmund Freud, and Richard Dawkins have all previously asserted that belief in God is a mental disorder. But the answer is no. First, although some brain disorders are sometimes associated with apparently religious features, these diseases are even more likely to trigger abnormal

---

1. Carrazana and Cheng, "St Theresa's Dart."

experiences of a non-religious nature. Furthermore, the fact that a brain disease can bring about a religious experience is no different from the production of auditory or visual hallucinations by similar processes. If, for example, a patient suffering an epileptic seizure hears things that are not real, we do not conclude that everything we hear is false. And when brain diseases create hallucinations of a quasi-religious nature, they do not usually give rise to beliefs and practices similar to religion. If we want to understand the neurobiological basis for religious experience, we need to focus on the normal brain.

There is a field of scientific inquiry that aims to characterize the brain mechanisms related to how we process, store, and apply information about other people. Known as social cognition, this area of psychology studies the mental processes involved in how we come to know about other people in the world around us. Brain imaging studies have shown that people use these mental processes when praying,[2] which is unsurprising given that people of faith commonly describe their experiences of God as being like a personal relationship. So perhaps there are specific brain processes involved in how we become aware of God.

If this were the case, as discussed in chapter 6, the weight of evidence for the authenticity of experiences of God would be increased by showing them to be compatible with experimental data that can be independently verified. It would also provide a basis for understanding how acts of public worship could bring about experiences of God. In other words, is it possible to identify scientific data and principles that can be combined with Christian thinking to provide a holistic model for an encounter with God?

Speaking in Tongues: A Model for Experiences of God?

Generally, experiences of God cannot be produced at will and are therefore difficult to study scientifically. But there is a religious experience that some people can trigger whenever they want—speaking in tongues, in which the individual appears to be speaking an unknown language. A Barna research poll found that between 7 percent and 13 percent of adult Christians have spoken in tongues.[3] It is therefore a common practice, but it also forms part of a network of experiences and concepts about God.

2. Schjoedt et al., "Power of Charisma."
3. Barna Group, "How Different Generations View and Engage."

The Bible makes several references to speaking in tongues, which was recognized in the early church as one of God's gifts. The ability to speak in tongues was often regarded as a sign of having received the Holy Spirit—that is, God as spiritually active in the world. St Paul referred to speaking in tongues as communicating with God with the spirit, distinguishing it from communication with the mind: "I will pray with the spirit and I will pray with the mind also; I will sing with the spirit and I will sing with the mind also" (1 Corinthians 14:15).

Furthermore, there is evidence that speaking in tongues can lead to improvements in well-being and can play an important role in changing the direction of the participants' lives. Thus, according to the evidence pyramid described in chapter 6, we can consider speaking in tongues to be level 2 evidence for an encounter with God. It has also been studied scientifically, albeit in a limited way.

Ms A. was a forty-four-year-old lady whose case was reported in the medical literature by Roy Reeves and colleagues from Jackson, USA.[4] Unlike the patient described at the beginning of this chapter, Ms A. had no previous or current history of neurological or mental illness. She was seeking medical advice about neck muscle tension and headaches. During the consultation, she mentioned that some of her friends at church were worried because they had noticed Ms A. jerked her left arm when she was speaking in tongues.

Routine blood tests were normal and, also unlike the patient above, an MRI scan of Ms A.'s brain was entirely normal. Nevertheless, Ms A. agreed to have the electrical activity within her brain recorded using electrodes placed on the scalp. This procedure is an established tool that can increase our understanding of how the brain works. It is also used medically to diagnose a number of ailments, such as epilepsy or conditions that can disturb sleep. For Ms A., the recordings were to be made while she prayed silently in tongues.

At first, the electrical activity in her brain was consistent with deep relaxation or light sleep, but after a few minutes electrical discharges were seen to arise from the right temporal lobe of her brain. When Ms A. stopped praying in tongues, the discharges also stopped. She repeated this process twice and each time she prayed in tongues the electrical discharges returned.

4. Reeves et al., "Temporal Lobe Discharges and Glossolalia."

In another study, Andrew Newberg and others from the University of Pennsylvania used medical imaging to see what was happening in the brain when people were speaking in tongues.[5] They recruited five women ranging from thirty-eight to fifty-two years who described themselves as a Christian in a Charismatic or Pentecostal tradition and had practiced speaking in tongues for more than five years. The researchers obtained images of brain blood flow during speaking in tongues and compared them to images taken while singing gospel songs. The subjects felt that their speaking in tongues was involuntary.

The main difference between these two conditions was that the blood flow to the frontal lobes was reduced while the subjects were speaking in tongues. The frontal lobes are known to be active during mental tasks that focus attention. The reduced frontal activity during speaking in tongues was therefore consistent with the subjects' reports of loss of voluntary control. It is worth noting that this finding is not consistent with faking, at least in the subjects examined, because intentional fabrication would be expected to increase frontal lobe activity. There were other changes in brain flow which the researchers thought may relate to differences in emotional activity between singing and speaking in tongues.

At one time, it was thought that speaking in tongues might be a form of epilepsy, and finding electrical discharges while speaking in tongues also suggests this possibility. The method researchers used to study brain blood flow during speaking in tongues is also used for patients with epilepsy as a means to locate the part of the brain that is causing the seizures. The technique uses a radioactive substance that is rapidly taken up in brain tissue depending on the blood flow to that region. The substance is fixed in the brain within a few minutes and remains there so that images of the brain can be taken later when the patient is no longer suffering a seizure, or no longer speaking in tongues. In patients with epilepsy, the part of the brain causing the seizures shows a marked increase in blood flow. However, this pattern was not seen when volunteers were speaking in tongues.

It has also been suggested that speaking in tongues might be a mental disorder. In fact, other research has shown that those who perform speaking in tongues have lower rates of mental illness.

There can be no doubt that what happens in our minds is intimately linked with the biological processes in our brains and bodies. The way in which a blow to the head can stop our mental processes altogether is an

5. Newberg et al., "Measurement of Regional Cerebral Blood Flow."

extreme example. So if God were to interact with the biological processes within our brains in a particular way, we might experience that as an encounter with God. A reduction in blood flow to the frontal lobes as seen when speaking in tongues may be a marker for a brain state which gives greater freedom for God to interact with neural processes, possibly because the mental activity that focuses our attention elsewhere has been switched off. Indeed, additional imaging studies have revealed other spiritual activities that are associated with a reduction in blood flow to the frontal lobes—for example, receiving prayer (as discussed further in chapter 12).

Although significant, these findings do not address the question of how God might act at the neural level. In the previous chapter, quantum uncertainty linked to a chaotic system was proposed as means by which God could drive evolution by natural selection without interrupting the laws of nature. Perhaps God could also use this mechanism to interact with nature more generally, including our brains.

Quantum Events in the Brain?

Recent scientific advances have shown that quantum coherence does not only happen under experimental conditions but also occurs within biological systems. It was previously thought electrons behaved as coherent waves only for very short distances or under extremely cold conditions, close to absolute zero. But it is now thought that quantum coherence occurs naturally in chlorophyll, the plant molecule that converts light into energy.[6] Electrons displaced by light photons hitting the chlorophyll pass through the molecule in this coherent way to the reaction center where the energy is passed on. The electron effectively passes along several paths at the same time, in the same way that electrons simultaneously pass through the two slits in the double-slit experiment described in previous chapters. It has been suggested that this process evolved under evolutionary pressures because it is a very fast method for transferring energy.

It has also been proposed, but not proven, that this sort of process can happen within the human brain. The brain is made up of neurons, and within these neurons are little microtubules which some researchers have put forward as routes for the rapid passage of energy by quantum coherence. The evidence supporting this idea includes the observation that the brain sometimes appears to act faster than can be accounted for by classical

6. Hameroff et al., "Quantum Effects."

transfer of electrons down neurons. It has also been suggested that, in the same way an electron can be in several positions at once when behaving as a wave, when we make a mental decision, we hold both options in our brain simultaneously. The moment of choosing only one option has been likened to the collapse of the quantum probability wave that occurs when the position of the electron is observed.

An ability for God to interact with electrons in a state of quantum coherence could feasibly enable God to influence the human mind. Yet, if quantum coherence were to be the only opportunity for God to interact with nature, the possibilities for influencing mental processes would be extremely limited. On the other hand, when linked to a chaotic system which is extremely sensitive to initial conditions, these minute influences could be amplified, leading to large-scale effects.

Chaos in the Brain

Chaotic systems are very common within nature, and that includes the human brain. Scientific analysis has shown that the brain's electrical activity exhibits chaotic properties in which the progression of the wave pattern over time will be sensitive to initial conditions. There is therefore the prospect that small changes occurring within the brain because of divine action at the quantum level can be amplified, resulting in significantly greater effects.

By using the mathematics of chaos theory, it is possible to measure the complexity of signals from different brain regions (roughly equivalent to determining the "priest's missional factor" illustrated in the previous chapter). This kind of analysis has been performed for brain electrical activity occurring during sleep, showing that electrical activity exhibits higher degrees of chaos when dreaming. And the Bible often depicts dream sleep as a moment for divine action. For instance, the Gospel of Matthew describes dreams in which an angel of the Lord visits Joseph, the legal father of Jesus, to pass on specific instructions and warnings of imminent danger (Matthew 1:20–25; 2:13–15).

But is speaking in tongues chaotic? The spikes in the brain electrical activity seen during speaking in tongues certainly represent an increase in complexity, although formal analysis for chaotic features has not been reported for speaking in tongues. On the other hand, researchers from the Indian Institute of Technology, Kharagpur, have used this kind of analysis to show that brain electrical activity demonstrates chaotic features when volunteers imagine themselves making isolated vowel sounds which have no linguistic meaning.[7] This activity may be related to speaking in tongues, which has been described as consisting of vowels that have a clear audio form but do not make sense. Typically, speaking in tongues also entails periods in which particular sounds are repeated, mirroring the way in which some chaotic time-series exhibit periods when the curves swing between two values. Rather than be the end-product of an encounter with God, speaking in tongues could be a sign that the brain is in a chaotic state that is sensitive to initial conditions. Such a state could increase the opportunity for God to interact with the mind in a way that cooperates with, rather than overrides, the natural processes occurring within the brain.

A Still, Small Voice

In a letter to the German physicist Max Born (a pioneer of quantum mechanics), Albert Einstein expressed his discomfort with the idea that randomness was a fundamental part of nature, by writing, "God does not play dice with the universe."[8] On the other hand, people of faith often feel that events that appear to happen by chance are linked in some way to a divine plan. God could act in ways that are hidden from us to determine the outcome of events that seem to be random. And this is not a new idea. In the Bible, when selecting a replacement for Judas, the apostles seem to accept that the casting of lots can provide an opportunity for God to act (Acts 1:23–26). Moreover, Jesus's calming of a storm (Luke 8:24) points to divine influence upon systems which we now know to be chaotic

To suggest that God uses chance and chaos to interact with our brains is therefore consistent with the network of experiences and theories that make up Christian thinking. Chance and chaos may be the foundation not only for speaking in tongues but also for other experiences of God. To work almost imperceptibly within natural processes may seem too subtle a way for God to communicate with us. But it is not uncommon for people of faith to experience God speaking in just this way, a sensation the Bible likens to a "still small voice" (1 Kings 19:12, RSV) or, in other translations "a sound of sheer silence" (NRSV) or "a low whisper" (ESV). And in the words of Christian philosopher of science Nancey Murphy, "God's action

---

7. Sikdar et al., "Chaos Analysis of Speech Imagery."

8. Born, *Born-Einstein Letters*, 91.

at the neural level might account for that still small voice that has long been taken to provide invitation to a fuller, freer life."[9]

9. Murphy, "Divine Action, Emergence, and Scientific Explanation."

12

Words of Worship

"THE APPEARANCES ARE CONSISTENT with a metastasis." Carol was giving her professional opinion at the weekly Multidisciplinary Team Meeting for the care of patients with cancer of the urinary tract and prostate. As a radiologist, Carol's role at the meeting was to report the key findings on X-rays and other medical imaging tests, in this case a CT scan from Mr Doherty, a patient with prostate cancer. She had noticed an area in the pelvis which could be a site where Mr Doherty's cancer had spread to the bone—a metastasis. If her suspicion was correct, Mr Doherty would no longer be a candidate for surgery.

Multidisciplinary Team Meetings struck Carol as being a kind of ritual. Everything happens in a prescribed order. A clinician describes the patient's medical history and the findings on examination, the pathologist demonstrates the appearances of tissue retrieved at a biopsy or surgery, the radiologist shows the scans and X-rays, and the whole team, which also includes surgeons, oncologists, nurses, and social workers, agrees on the best treatment for each individual patient. The whole process is documented in detail. Yet this formalized structure probably contributes to the effectiveness of such meetings. Research has shown that the use of Multidisciplinary Team Meeting increases the average survival of cancer patients, in many cases by more than some anti-cancer drugs.

Carol had chosen her words carefully. She could have said "diagnostic of" or "suspicious of" rather than "consistent with" a metastasis. However, her years of training and experience in translating images into written language had taught her that each of these phrases conveys a different probability for the abnormality being cancer. "Diagnostic of" was too definite, whereas "suspicious of" might not be enough for the team to recommend further investigation which, in Carol's opinion, was the best option. To just assume that Mr Doherty's bone lesion was cancer might mean the benefits of surgery would be lost if in fact the abnormality turned out to be something else. On the other hand, if it were a metastasis, surgery would be inappropriate.

After further discussion, the team recommended that Mr Doherty should have a PET scan, and if that showed no other abnormalities, he should have a biopsy of the affected bone.

If the exact words chosen to describe a CT scan can have such an impact on the thoughts and actions of a multidisciplinary team, then it is unsurprising that the way words are spoken during public worship can have a great impact on the congregation of worshippers.

It is important to note that the emphasis is on the way worship affects the participants. It is all too easy to imagine that the words spoken during public worship are formulas intended to manipulate supernatural forces with the hope of bringing about particular effects on certain people or objects. The apparent obligation to say things in unison and aloud are just some of the factors that can add to this impression. But Christian worship is far from a magical rite designed to manipulate God. Although the words and phrases used in churches have developed over many centuries through trial and error, they can be easier to follow if we take into account the results of recent scientific studies into the mental processes that accompany religious experience but reinterpreted in a framework that allows for the existence of God. And by looking for interpretations that work across multiple levels of the evidence pyramid, we can make sure that the scientific principles of evidence evaluation are being followed. When we do this, we discover that the way in which our brains and bodies respond to words during worship is affected not only by whether they are said silently or out loud, alone or together, but also by whether we are speaking or listening, by what we think of the person speaking, and even where in the room the words are coming from.

For example, worshippers might speak of God as being "in the highest" or that he "came down from heaven." But isn't it foolish and unscientific to think that God can be found in the sky? Yet neuroscience has shown these phrases are not simply unsophisticated ways to communicate abstract ideas about God. In fact, thinking about concepts for God is fundamentally interlinked with brain activity that is related to the processing of spatial information. When we reflect on the divine, we also think about vertical position in space.[1] To put it another way, our brains associate God with highness.

In an attempt to find concepts for God that are less contradictory to science, we might consider using phrases with no spatial information at all, by removing "in the highest" altogether, for instance. Or we might use an unspecified location in space, replacing "came down from heaven" with something such as "entered the universe." But then we would lose the benefits gained from how vertical position helps people to respond to God by connecting the mental images we have for God to everyday body-based experiences. A new mental image may be better in one respect but worse in another.

Studies have also shown that people respond more quickly to and are more likely to recall God-related concepts when they are presented higher in visual space.[2] The tradition whereby preachers address their congregations from an elevated platform known as the pulpit is likely to have corresponding advantages. Research data also shows that when people encounter God-related words, their visual attention is systematically shifted upwards.[3] The higher locations within places of worship often contain visual features that stand out from their background (for example, stars on the ceiling). Although chosen for symbolic reasons, the upward shift in visual awareness prompted by hearing God-related words can draw worshippers' attention to these features and, in so doing, bring about physiological changes with a range of benefits that are described more fully in the next chapter.

Narrative

Storytelling plays a key role in human culture. Stories shape human experience and empower the transmission of social values. It is therefore unsurprising that narrative should be an important part of Christian worship. The retelling of parables that Jesus used to prompt an encounter with truth and meaning is a good example. But narrative plays a much bigger role in public worship. A church service is not only about the congregation expressing their religious convictions. Worshippers should also be changed by the experience, and narrative is central to this formative role. As Calvin University Professor James K. A. Smith highlights in his book, *Imagining*

1. Meier et al., "What's 'Up' with God?," 699.
2. Meier et al., "God Is Up?"
3. Chasteen et al., "Thinking of God Moves Attention."

the Kingdom: How Worship Works, "The overall narrative arc of Christian worship—gathering, confessing, listening, submitting, communing, sending—tells a story in the background by its very structure and organization." Smith argues that the Story enacted in our communal worship reshapes our minds and changes our behavior more effectively than intellectual assent to a set of beliefs.[4] The Christian story is complex and many-layered. It is hard, if not impossible, to compress this narrative into a single sentence but we can try to do so by using the words of Rowan Williams and Nancey Murphy quoted in earlier chapters: There was one particular historical community who experienced God with increasing intensity until he came among them in the person of Jesus, who now invites us all to a freer and fuller life through a renewed relationship with God.[5]

The ability of narrative to change attitudes and behavior has become a focus for scientific research. For example, in health communication, it has been shown that narratives can be persuasive when encouraging lifestyle changes that lower the risk of disease.[6] The lessons learnt from the scientific study of narrative may therefore help us to understand why certain patterns of words used during worship might be more likely to change attitudes and behaviors towards God.

Some researchers have considered how the basic features of the language used in narratives could be modified for greater persuasiveness. One aspect of language, known as agency, relates to who or what is bringing about the desired effect. In health communication, several studies have shown that changing agency can affect people's perceptions of health threats. In one study, participants rated their susceptibility to colon cancer higher when agency was assigned to people (e.g., many people acquire colon cancer) rather than to cancer (e.g., colon cancer strikes many people).[7]

It is also possible to change the perspective of the person or persons involved. When a person or group is describing their personal experience in a direct way, it is known as first-person narration (e.g., we did it; it happened to us). A second-person point of view casts the reader(s) as the central character (e.g., you did it; it happened to you). With a third-person narrative, the event is described by someone who is not directly

---

4. Smith, *Imagining the Kingdom*, 173.

5. Williams, *Ray of Darkness*, 102–103; Murphy, "Divine Action, Emergence and Scientific Explanation," 258.

6. Shen et al., "Impact of Narratives on Persuasion."

7. Chen et al., "Persuasive Effects of Linguistic Agency Assignments."

involved (e.g., they did it; it happened to them.) In health communication, there seems to be little difference between the impact of first- and third-person perspectives. Because it is used less frequently, there is little research data on the impact of the second-person perspective. However, there is some evidence to suggest that second-person narratives trigger a greater emotional response.[8]

Both agency and point of view are easily modified for the narratives used in worship. For example, worship services often include a declaration that behaviors damaging to relationship with God (i.e., sins) have been forgiven. This announcement (called the Absolution) follows a confession, and these acts are both essential to the renewal of one's relationship with God, which is part of the overarching worship narrative. As shown in the table below, the Absolution can be made with agency assigned to the worshippers or to God, and in each of the three perspectives.

	Agency assigned to worshippers	Agency assigned to God
First person	We receive God's forgiveness.	God gives us his forgiveness.
Second person	You receive God's forgiveness.	God gives you his forgiveness.
Third person	The congregation receives God's forgiveness	God gives the congregation his forgiveness.

Table 3: Six possible descriptions of the Absolution

Some churches have authorized particular forms of words for this part of the service. An example from the Church of England is:

Almighty God,
who forgives all who truly repent,
have mercy upon *you*,
pardon and deliver *you* from all *your* sins,
confirm and strengthen *you* in all goodness,
and keep *you* in life eternal.[9]

This form of words assigns agency to God, using a second-person perspective. However, the guidance goes on to state that either a "you" or an "us" form can be used (words in italics indicate the points where changes

8. Wei, "Exploring the Effects of Interactive Narratives."
9. Church of England, "Prayer and Worship Resources."

may be necessary), although those who are not ordained priests are not meant to use the "you" form.

Research has shown that changing the perspective can have a significant impact on how people respond to language. The first- and third-person points of view tend to promote an observer's perspective, while the use of "you" fosters the development of memories and enhances emotional response. Despite this data, the issue of perspective in the phrases used during worship seems to have received little or no attention. In fact, for the Absolution above, the Church of England guidance says that "the printing of any of these absolutions in either the 'you' or 'us' form has no doctrinal or other significance."[10]

So does it matter which words are used? Although there have been no studies specifically looking at the impact of "you" forms in worship, narrative research suggests that with second-person language (the "you" form), the congregation may be more likely to feel that they are experiencing the event. As discussed in chapter 5, the principles of evidence evaluation indicate that the decisions should be based on best available evidence and, until further research is conducted, preference for the "you" form would seem justified.

Giving and Receiving Prayer

The Absolution described above is a moment during worship when the congregation are the recipients of a prayer said by the worship leader. Another example is the Blessing, which takes place just before the congregation are sent out. At other times, the worshippers are saying the prayers, often structured prayers spoken in unison, but sometimes silent private prayers.

Brain imaging research led by Uffe Schjoedt from Aarhus University, Denmark, suggests that each of these types of prayer is associated with a different pattern of brain activity. One study imaged the brains of Christian and non-religious volunteers while they were receiving pre-recorded prayers for healing.[11] Typically, the prayers assigned agency to God but were spoken using a third-person perspective. However, from the context, it was clear that the prayer was intended for the volunteer (e.g., "Please let your mercy and rich blessing enter this person and bring healing to his life"). The researchers wanted to see whether assumptions about the

10. Church of England, "Prayer and Worship Resources."
11. Schjoedt et al., "Power of Charisma."

speaker's influential authority (which the researchers called "charisma") would have an effect on brain activity while listening to the prayers. So, before each prayer, the participants were told that the person praying was either a non-Christian, a Christian, or a Christian known for his healing powers. In fact, the three speakers were all "ordinary" Christians randomly allocated to each category.

For the non-religious volunteers, the speaker's religious status made no difference to the patterns of brain activity. However, the Christian participants showed lower levels of activity in the frontal lobes of the brain in response to prayers spoken by a Christian known for his healing powers but increased activation when listening to a non-Christian speaker. Furthermore, the participants reported a greater sense of God's presence when frontal lobe activity was reduced. Based on brain imaging studies performed during speaking in tongues, the previous chapter considered whether reduced activity in the frontal lobes could be a marker for a brain state which allows God to interact with neural processes. The above findings suggest that receipt of prayer may be a similar situation. Words and phrases that can reduce activity in the frontal lobes of the brain may therefore be advantageous for inducing a greater experience of God's presence while potentially providing opportunities for God to interact with neural processes. One way to achieve this effect would be to include occasions when the worship leader prays for the congregation, especially when the person praying is perceived to have greater influential authority. (This provides an additional reason for using the "you" form of the Absolution outlined because only ordained priests can use this form of words.)

Joint Speech

It is common for public worship to include moments when the members of the congregation say things together. Examples include collective prayer and the joint recitation of the Creed. To some, these moments can seem a bit strange, rather like recanting magic spells. So what, if anything, does this joint speech achieve?

We can begin to answer this question by considering the results of a brain imaging study performed at University College London. Using functional magnetic resonance scanning, the researchers looked at what happens in the brain when two people speak sentences synchronously with each other. Participants synchronized their speech with either the experimenter's live voice in real time or with a pre-recorded version. However, the participants had not been told that recorded voices would be used. The study results were remarkable because they showed differences in brain activity between joint speech with a live voice as compared to joint speech with a recording.[12]

Located in the temporal lobe at the side of your brain (usually the opposite side to the dominant hand), there is an area known as the auditory cortex. This brain region is key for hearing and understanding speech, and without it we could not recognize language. Normally, when we are speaking ourselves, activity within the speech-responsive temporal cortex is suppressed. This is thought to be the way in which we can tell the difference between our own speech and that coming from someone else. In the brain imaging study outlined above, suppression of the temporal cortex was seen when participants synchronized their speech with a recording, but not when the voice was live. With a live voice, the auditory cortex responded as though the participant were simply listening, and not speaking.

This finding has an important implication for the use of joint speech in public worship (when live). When we pray collectively, our brains respond as though someone else is praying. As we have seen, our brains respond very differently when we receive prayer as compared to praying ourselves. The effects associated with receiving prayer as outlined above may therefore also apply to collective prayer.

Priming

Science also shows us how certain words can have a negative impact on worship. A well-known study by Canadian psychologists Will M. Gervais and Ara Norenzayan found that encountering the words "analyze," "reason," "ponder," "think," and "rational" reduced the participants' confidence in the existence of God (in comparison to an identical control activity that used the words "hammer," "shoes," "jump," "retrace," and "brown" instead). The effects were seen irrespective of whether the participants were religious or non-religious.[13]

But why should certain words encourage religious disbelief? The researchers say that these words trigger an analytical way of thinking which, for some people, reduces their confidence in the existence of God. And

12. Jasmin et al., "Cohesion and Joint Speech."

13. Gervais and Norenzayan, "Analytic Thinking Promotes Religious Disbelief."

there are many other triggers for analytical thinking that can have the same effect. Similar results were found in response to an image of artwork depicting a reflective thinking pose (Rodin's "The Thinker"). Even words printed in a font that is difficult to read can trigger analytical thinking and promote religious disbelief.

When exposure to a stimulus influences how someone responds later to a related stimulus without conscious guidance or intention, it is known within cognitive psychology as "priming." Priming effects are temporary. Research has not yet determined how long the influence of analytical thinking on religious belief lasts, but priming effects typically go on for between fifteen and thirty minutes (sometimes longer). People of faith therefore need not avoid analytical thinking in general. In fact, Christian's are urged to "gird up" their minds (1 Peter 1:13); in other words, prepare their minds for action and hard work. Moreover, people who are accustomed to thinking analytically about their faith appear to be immune to the priming effects described above, as suggested by a study led by Julie Yonker of Calvin University, Michigan. When participants were recruited from a Christian University, triggers for analytical thinking were found to increase confidence in the existence of God, contrary to Gervais's and Norenzayan's original findings.[14]

Analytical thinking is one side of a concept known as the dual processing theory. Thoughts can also arise by non-analytical processes, also called intuitive thinking. Intuitive thinking (sometimes known as Type 1) is fast, automatic, and largely non-conscious, whereas analytical thinking (Type 2) is abstract, rule-based, and primarily conscious. By way of illustration, consider these questions:

- At St Peter's Church, the Sunday morning service is immediately followed by coffee. Together, the service and coffee last for one hour and twenty minutes. The service lasts for one hour longer than the coffee. How long does the coffee last?

- The new pastor at St Mary's Church was so popular that the size of the congregation doubled every week. After eight weeks, the church was completely full. How many weeks did it take for the church to be half full?

- Volunteers at St John's Church are making palm crosses for next Sunday's church services. If it takes five volunteers five minutes to

14. Yonker et al., "Primed Analytic Thought and Religiosity."

make five crosses, how long would it take twenty volunteers to make twenty crosses?

If you used analytical (Type 2) thinking, you probably answered, "Ten minutes," Seven weeks," and, "Five minutes" (which are the correct answers). However, many people are naturally inclined towards intuitive thinking, and if you answered, "Twenty minutes," "Four weeks," and, "Twenty minutes" respectively, you may be one of them. On the other hand, if you are a regular churchgoer, it is possible that the religious context of the questions activated intuitive thinking owing to a priming effect (similar but opposite to those words above that decreased confidence in God). A study led by American neuroscientist Joshua D. Greene found that it was possible to experimentally induce a mindset that favors intuitive thinking by asking participants to write about a time when following their intuition/first instinct resulted in a good outcome. Furthermore, these participants subsequently reported stronger belief in God compared to participants who wrote about an experience that supported analytical thinking.[15]

It may be tempting to suppose that analytical thinking is generally better than intuitive thinking for decision-making, but this is not the case. The key is to match the thinking mode to the characteristics of the task in hand. Analytical thinking is more reliable for quantitative problems with objective measures and clear organizing principles. Intuitive thinking works best for unquantifiable problems with an emotional aspect for which organizing principles are unavailable and where it is possible to draw on previous experience. Analytical processes may be best for mathematical problems (like the question about the half-full church above), but perhaps less useful when deciding whether to trust someone.

Research suggests that doctors rely on both processes when making diagnostic decisions. Even with their extensive scientific training, doctors tend to use intuitive processes for an initial evaluation, reserving analytical thinking for more complex diagnostic problems. The main brain regions involved in analytical thinking are the frontal lobes. We see this, for example, in a brain imaging study led by Pam Hruska of the University of Calgary, Canada. Using Magnetic Resonance Imaging to look at the brains of doctors when making clinical decisions, the study found the greatest activation of

15. Shenhav et al., "Divine Intuition."

the frontal lobes occurred when the doctors were reviewing hard clinical cases which required analytical thinking.[16]

Interestingly, some modern worship songs contain words from the list that was found to promote disbelief by triggering analytical thinking. Yet analytical thinking may be disadvantageous during worship. Worship is meant to boost commitment to God, not reduce confidence in his existence! Studies have shown a link between religious belief and intuitive thinking and, given the characteristics of intuitive tasks outlined above, intuitive approaches are likely to be more appropriate when processing the God-related experiences that underlie worship. As C.S. Lewis points out, Christian teaching cannot be grasped by the intellect alone, even if we "might have expected, we may think we should have preferred, an unrefracted light giving us ultimate truths in systematic form—something we could have tabulated and memorised and relied on like the multiplication table."[17]

We should therefore expect to find within public, worship activities that are likely to suppress analytical thinking while promoting intuitive modes. Clearly, these patterns of worship would not have been adopted based on a knowledge of dual process theory, but they may have emerged over time as more effective ways of worshipping, and we can apply modern science to corroborate these approaches.

Refocusing the Frontal Lobes

The reduction in frontal lobe activity when receiving prayer, especially when the speaker is thought to have influential authority, would not only increase participants' susceptibility to authoritative narratives but also inhibit analytical thinking. Activation of the frontal lobes can also be minimized with appropriate priming. But Schjoedt and colleagues have proposed a third mechanism by which frontal lobe activity can be altered during religious interactions (figure 6).[18] The concept is founded on the idea that there is a limit to the brain's capacity for thought. There is only so much that our brains can process at one time. So if the brain is occupied by something else, there will be insufficient cognitive resources left for analytical thinking. One way this can happen is when people observe or take part in rituals.

16. Hruska et al., "Hemispheric Activation Differences,"
17. Lewis, *Reflections on the Psalms*, 88.
18. Schjoedt et al., "Cognitive Resource Depletion in Religious Interactions."

Research tells us that our brains process actions by breaking them down into smaller units which are then built into a mental picture where the causal connections between units and overall intent of the action are clear. For example, a worship service often involves the priest drinking wine from a chalice in commemoration of the last meal Jesus shared with his disciples before his Crucifixion. "Grasping chalice," "lifting chalice," and "opening mouth" are low-level units that our brains can easily and automatically link together into a meaningful action sequence where the goal is "drinking wine."

But what if the action were part of a ritual where the sequence was "grasping chalice," "lifting chalice above head," "lowering chalice to chest height," "moving chalice to right," "moving chalice to left," "replacing chalice on altar"? And what if the chalice were extravagantly adorned with gems and symbols that seemed to have no particular relevance to drinking wine? In these circumstances, the way the actions link together and their overall purpose are much less clear. This ambiguity seems to make it harder for our brains to link the low-level units together and identify the intended goal. The brain has to refocus its attention on processing the ritual actions, and the additional mental effort involved limits the worshipper's capacity for analytical thinking, making them more open to the religious narrative that accompanies the ritual. Interestingly, research data suggests these effects persist even if the ritual becomes familiar through regular practice.

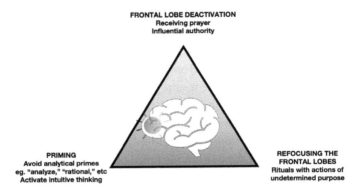

Figure 6: Mechanisms by which acts of worship can affect
the frontal lobes of the brain

A skeptic might see the use of ritual described above as a kind of trick that helps to transmit a false or even dangerous worldview. But rituals are also used in secular contexts (such as university graduation ceremonies), and their effects on beliefs and behaviors will be determined by the accompanying narrative. On the other hand, some Christians may also be suspicious of rituals, concerned that they may become an end in their own right or be thought of as a way to gain favor with God.

Ritualism of this sort is a real trap into which people have fallen for millennia. Yet by reinterpreting the science of religious action in a Christian context, it is possible to see worship rituals as useful tools for supporting the communication of the Christian narrative and bringing people closer to God. The analysis above points to the increased power of words when combined with ritual. But, as we shall see in the next chapter, ritual actions have additional benefits of their own.

13

Hearts and Minds

BILL HAS ARRIVED AT the Nuclear Medicine department of his local hospital. He's been here before, when he had a scan that showed blockages in the arteries to his heart. This time he's come for another heart scan, but a different kind. This scan will assess the nerves that supply his heart. At first, he was surprised to hear that the heart had any nerves, but then he remembered the occasions when he had felt pain from his heart, so he supposed that there must be nerves in his heart for him to feel that. And he was also reminded of his nephew George who was seriously into competitive archery. His trainer had taught him to be aware of his heartbeat so that he could release the arrow between heartbeats. Apparently, the tiniest movement from his beating heart could deflect the arrow just enough to miss the center of the target. So maybe it is these cardiac nerves that allow George to sense his heartbeat.

A few months ago, the blockages in Bill's arteries caused a heart attack, and even now he tends to get breathless because his heart muscles have been weakened. His doctor said this means there is a risk that he could develop a dangerously abnormal heart rhythm, especially if the nerves to his heart are not working properly. If the latest Nuclear Medicine test (called an MIBG cardiac scan) shows that this is the case, they will advise him to have a small device placed under the skin just below his collarbone. Should he develop an abnormal heart rhythm, the device would correct it by sending electrical pulses to his heart.

The nerves to the heart that Bill's doctor is investigating are part of a body control network known as the autonomic nervous system, a section of the nervous system that unconsciously regulates physiological processes such as heart rate, blood pressure, and breathing. The autonomic nervous system has two major divisions, called the sympathetic and parasympathetic. The sympathetic system brings about the "fear, fight, or flight" response to threats, while parasympathetic activity can be summarized by "rest and digest." For people like Bill, who have a weak heart, abnormal functioning of the autonomic nervous system, especially imbalance between the sympathetic and parasympathetic components, can lead to harmful changes in the size, shape, and structure of the heart, which result in further weakening and a tendency to develop dangerous changes in heart rhythm.

Worship and the Autonomic Nervous System

People often ask why Christian worship involves so many different postures and movements, such as kneeling and bowing the head. Newcomers to worship can find these actions off-putting, and even some Christians question whether they are really necessary. But scientific data suggests that bodily actions performed during worship are not arbitrary customs adopted only for their symbolic meaning. These actions also have effects on how our body works, altering physiological processes such as blood pressure, heart rate, and breathing. In turn, these processes influence our emotions, thoughts, and decision-making. Simply assigning sacred meaning to arm movements can lead to greater experiences of positive emotions and a sense of relating to something greater than self.[1] Such responses tend to happen automatically, without having to be learned, so that certain bodily postures and actions pair naturally with particular thoughts and feelings. As Patty Van Cappellen, Director of the Belief, Affect & Behavior Laboratory at Duke University, explains, "The locus of religion is not only in the mind or in the brain but in the full body."[2] And the regulation of the autonomic nervous system so important for Bill's health also plays a key role in the physical aspects of worship.

Modern scientific research has shown that spiritual practices are frequently associated with changes in the autonomic nervous system, especially simultaneous activation of sympathetic and parasympathetic divisions.[3] Many activities that can form part of mainstream Christian worship are highly likely to affect autonomic function (see table 4), and similar behaviors are found in other religions. Changes in the autonomic nervous

1. Freeburg et al., "Meaning Behind the Movement."
2. Van Cappellen and Edwards, "Embodiment of Worship."
3. Newberg, *Principles of Neurotheology*, 160–61.

system are also associated with human emotions, including those that may be experienced during worship. For example, awe is associated with changes in both sympathetic and parasympathetic components.

Novel or significant stimuli are important factors that increase the activity of the autonomic nervous system, prompting a reaction known as the orienting response. An example from the natural world is the way a herd of grazing deer will all look up in the presence of a possible predator. An initial phase of information gathering involves dilation of the pupil of the eye under the influence of the sympathetic system, combined with a slowing of the heart rate that is driven by parasympathetic activity. If the trigger for the orienting response indicates a need for immediate action, the sympathetic system takes over completely, increasing heart rate, breathing, and muscle blood flow in readiness for running away from or confronting the threat. Once the threat has passed, parasympathetic activity resumes, returning the heart rate and breathing to normal. In higher animals and humans, the close relationship between the autonomic nervous system and the brain means that the orienting response not only alters physiological processes but is associated with mental and emotional changes as well. The mind becomes more alert as it attends to and evaluates the importance of the event that triggered the response and gets ready to respond.

A number of worship actions can bring about an orienting response. Examples include changes in posture, such as standing from a kneeling position, bowing and raising the head, and genuflection (lowering the body briefly by bending one knee to the ground). Tracking movement or sound can also trigger an orienting response, such as opening your eyes after having them closed for a period, watching people move in procession, hearing an unexpected noise such as a bell, or seeing an incense burner swinging on its chain.

Some features of religious worship can prolong or intensify the orienting response and associated autonomic effects. One of these is the emotion of respect which may be experienced when the stimulus for the orienting response is a person one would follow carefully in order to learn something.[4] Greater attention may be drawn to particular people of respect, such as priests or bishops, by the ceremonial clothing they wear and/or an object they carry, for example a bishop's crook.

Research has also shown that the orienting response may be enhanced by features within our surroundings. For example, an imaging

4. Kondoh et al., "Experiencing Respect Elongates the Orienting Response."

study of brain activity while volunteers were looking for target objects in a range of virtual environments showed that brain responses were increased when seeking a target in an environment predominantly composed of vertical lines.[5] Worshipping within religious buildings with multiple vertical lines, for example columns and pillars, can potentially increase the effects of the orienting response. Performance of worship in other environments containing vertical lines, such as woodlands and forests, is likely to produce similar effects.

Activity	Autonomic Division	Examples
Change in posture	Sympathetic (orienting response)	Standing from kneeling position Genuflection Bowing head
Tracking movement	Sympathetic (orienting response)	Eyes closed to open Processions: e.g. entrance, gospel Swinging thurible
Tracking sound	Sympathetic (orienting response)	Sanctuary bell (esp. if hidden)
Music	Sympathetic	High frequency, fast
	Parasympathetic	Low frequency, slow
Repetition (movement, sound, music, speech)	Parasympathetic	Taizé worship, Contemplative Prayer
Group singing/chanting	Parasympathetic	
Unusual smell	Sympathetic & Parasympathetic	Incense
Unusual taste	Sympathetic & Parasympathetic	Communion wine

Table 4: Activities during religious worship and their likely effect on the autonomic nervous system

Glossary:

- *Genuflection*—Lowering the body briefly by bending one knee to the ground.

5. Sutton et al., "Geometry Three Ways."

- *Gospel procession*—Taking the Bible to the midst of the congregation before reading.

- *Thurible*—Incense burner suspended on a chain or chains.

- *Sanctuary bell*—A bell rung near the altar during the commemoration of the Last Supper.

- *Taizé*—A style of Christian worship that emphasizes stillness and repetitive singing.

- *Contemplative prayer*—Prayer that focuses the mind by constant repetition of a word or phrase.

Parasympathetic activity can be increased by taking up an erect posture with an expanded torso and limbs spread away from the body.[6] The same posture can also boost positive emotions such as gladness, hope, pride, and love. Another common trigger for the parasympathetic system is the repetition of movements, sounds, speech, or music. Repetition is an important part of certain religious practices, such as Taizé worship which emphasizes stillness and repetitive singing. Another example is contemplative prayer (including Rosary prayer), which focuses the mind by constant repetition of a word or phrase.[7] Group singing or chanting will also promote parasympathetic activity. Music can have a similar effect if it is slow and low pitched, but fast, high-pitched music will switch on the sympathetic system.

Some Christians may feel uncomfortable about the use of repetition in worship. Jesus warned against the use of "vain repetitions" in prayer in the hope that this would increase the chance of being heard by God (Matt 6:7, KJV). Repeating phrases and actions may also seem to be more like a magic spell than a prayer. But the repetitions described above are not performed with the intention of impressing or manipulating God. Rather, they aim to allow the participant to be affected by worship more readily. Historically, the view of worship has been not only about what we offer to God but also about how we are changed in the process.

When an action that stimulates the sympathetic division is performed at the same time as one that stimulates the parasympathetic, a combined autonomic response can be achieved. Possible combinations include the ringing of a bell during quiet, slow music or tracking of movement during group singing. Unusual smells or tastes will produce

---

6. Van Cappellen et al., "Bodily Feedback."

7. Bernardi et al., "Effect of Rosary Prayer."

a combined response on their own. Incense and communion wine are examples from Christian worship.

Bodily actions during worship may affect participants differently. Van Cappellen and Edwards have identified a range of factors that can potentially increase or diminish the effects of postures and other worship activities.[8] The physiological responses to postures and actions can be affected by whether or not the worshipper is being observed, which may be particularly relevant to certain forms of online worship (see chapter 16). Other influencing factors include the context—for example, secular versus religious, past exposure and experience of the posture or action, and the sensitivity of an individual's mind to bodily sensations. The worshipper's concept of God (e.g., loving versus authoritarian) may also play a role.

Why do so many acts of worship switch on the autonomic nervous system? Are these changes incidental by-products of spiritual practices that reflect faith-based thinking, or might they serve a function in their own right? Many worship practices have been developed over hundreds of years through trial and error. Successful practices have been preserved and adopted into tradition, while ineffective activities have been discarded. Worship actions that are effective because they trigger autonomic responses are likely to have been selected and passed on. Depending on the kind of worship one is used to, some of these activities may at first seem unnecessary or distracting. But a combined scientific/faith-based account of how these actions can have a positive impact may increase their acceptability. Some of these beneficial outcomes are discussed below and in the following chapter. Newer forms of worship can also potentially activate the autonomic nervous system in similar ways. Conversely, some churches have adopted patterns of worship that leave out actions that trigger autonomic activity, perhaps with the intention of simplifying public worship to make it more accessible. Such changes may ultimately prove counterproductive.

Health and Well-being

There is a large body of scientific evidence showing that people who regularly take part in religious worship have better physical and mental health. As discussed in chapter 5, a systematic review of several studies is considered to provide the highest level of evidence within medicine. Berkeley Professor of Public Health, Doug Oman, has reviewed more

8. Van Cappellen and Edwards, "Embodiment of Worship."

than a hundred studies looking at the relationship between religion and health.[9] The studies were published in eighty-three different journals and collectively authored by more than two hundred individuals. Applying the Bradford-Hill criteria we considered in chapters 1 and 3, Oman concluded that there was compelling evidence for religion and spirituality being not only associated with but also a *cause* for better health.

These studies have shown that active religious participation is associated with fewer hospital admissions, shorter hospital stays, and a reduction in death rate from any cause of up to 30 percent. Research focusing on heart disease in particular has demonstrated healthier blood pressure measurements and reduced rates of fatal heart attacks among religious individuals. Religious practice is also associated with better mental health, including lower rates of depression and anxiety.

The activities that form part of worship contribute to these improved health outcomes by modifying the functioning of the autonomic nervous system. Prayer has been linked with higher levels of cardiac autonomic control, which in turn is associated with a reduced risk of cardiac events and death from heart disease.[10] The controlled breathing needed for singing or speaking in groups can lead to reductions in blood pressure. Worship actions that change the internal physiological state of the body can also influence mental processes and emotions in a way that boosts mental health.

The increased social support found within religious communities is another factor that may contribute to the health benefits arising from religious participation. But worship actions are also relevant here. When people perform worship activities together, the resulting changes in physiology become synchronized, which in turn promotes social bonding and greater cohesion within the group.

Memory

Religious concepts can be abstract and difficult to grasp. Concepts that are tied to actions are easier to remember because people are better at retaining ideas that are expressed in multiple ways. The autonomic effects of these actions can also influence memory. Retention of memories is better when there are corresponding changes in physiological processes, such as heart rate response and the electrical conductivity of the skin. Medications that boost

9. Oman, *Why Religion and Spirituality Matter for Public Health.*

10. Tolentino and Bedirian, "Cardiac Autonomic Modulation Related to Prayer."

sympathetic action are known to enhance memory, and worship actions that switch on sympathetic activity are likely to have the same impact.

Openness to God

"When God breaks in, my picture of what it is to be me, and my attitudes to that picture, have been deeply disturbed and confused," writes Rowan Williams, the former Archbishop of Canterbury.[11] Whether brought on by worship or other spiritual practices, experiences of God often involve an altered sense of self, with a blurring of the boundary between self and the external world. According to a longstanding concept within neuroscience, the mental images we have of ourselves are based on information about our internal body and its interaction with its surroundings. The autonomic nervous system plays a key role in conveying this information to the brain, and an imbalance within the autonomic system can be associated with a disturbance in the sense of self.[12]

In chapters 10 and 11, we considered how quantum uncertainty linked with a chaotic system could be one way in which God interacts with his creation without interrupting the laws of nature. We might perceive this mode of God's cooperation with our brains as a "still small voice," as described in the Bible (1 Kings 19:12). By analyzing heart rate variability, studies have shown that the autonomic nervous system also exhibits chaotic properties with sensitivity to initial conditions. Worship actions that increase chaos within the autonomic nervous system could therefore potentially make worshippers more open to this kind of divine action. In fact, maneuvers such as changes in posture and slow breathing have been shown to change the complexity of heart rate variability.[13] A disturbance of the sense of self during worship or other spiritual practice could therefore be a signature of God acting in this way.

Body and Mind Working Together

It may be tempting to think that worship services should mainly aim to influence the mind. By having their minds filled with Christian thoughts

---

11. Williams, *Ray of Darkness*, 101.
12. Critchley et al., "Interaction Between Cognition, Emotion."
13. Radhakrishna et al., "Nonlinear Measures of Heart Rate Time Series."

and beliefs, people will hopefully be motivated to act rightly. Some may therefore see actions of the body as less important or even optional. For others, this view of worship may reflect a belief that, after death, an immaterial part of us (mind/soul) escapes the world and goes to a purely spiritual heaven. Therefore, worship need only address this immaterial aspect. But to diminish worship in this way is neither biblical nor scientific. As New Testament scholar N. T. Wright points out, "The story of all four gospels is not the story of how God came in Jesus to rescue souls for a disembodied, other-worldly heaven."[14] The Bible unmistakably points to a bodily resurrection in which the whole human being will live in a newly created Earth. And when St Paul writes about worship, he clearly sees worship as an activity that involves the body and the mind working together (e.g., Romans 12:1–2).

Paul's assessment is supported by current neuroscience which recognizes how the body, and the body's interaction with its surroundings, plays a key role in a wide range of mental processes. Not only are thoughts and emotions expressed in states of the body, but bodily states can also affect people's emotional and mental processes. In the context of worship, studies have demonstrated the effects of specific postures on religious thoughts and emotions. Different postures have been found to relate to prayer themes and emotional content in particular ways. Prayers made in an upright position are more likely to be focused on others, and people are more likely to experience positive emotions when they pray with hands raised and looking up.

Canadian–American philosopher James K. A. Smith has argued that our behavior is shaped more by bodily responses than by intellectual ideas.[15] Research has demonstrated that people do not consciously think about most of what they do, and their stated beliefs are often inconsistent with their actual behavior. Human behavior largely consists of embodied reactions to environmental stimuli—reactions that have developed through a long history of social interactions. Conscious reflection is involved but plays a lesser role than we might suppose. If selected appropriately, the actions performed during Christian worship services can shape the unconscious bodily reactions that will drive behaviors consistent with the Christian message, especially when undertaken in the context of a corresponding narrative (as discussed in the previous chapter).

---

14. Wright, "Mind, Spirit, Soul and Body."

15. Smith, *Imagining the Kingdom*.

But what about belief in God itself? Does that not require an intellectual evaluation of competing ideas about the nature of reality? As we shall see in the next chapter, the autonomic nervous system even plays a role in the formation of beliefs, including belief in the existence God.

− 14 −

Unbelief

AT MEDICAL SCHOOL, I heard a story about a student doctor whose colleagues had blocked the tubes of his stethoscope as a prank. Despite going through the whole of his training without ever hearing a single heart murmur or breath sound, he managed to pass his examinations and qualify as a doctor. Like many stories told at medical school, I suspect this one was only partly true at best and was retold to put across the idea that, although useful, the stethoscope may not be as important as you might think. Given the availability of new diagnostic technologies, this is probably truer today than it was then.

In the wrong hands (or ears), a stethoscope with blocked tubes could lead to a wrong diagnosis. Imagine this fictional scenario; John, a fifty-nine-year-old, overweight taxi driver, was sent to hospital because he had been unwell for a couple of weeks with a high temperature and a cough that produced green phlegm. Recently, he had developed pain in his right chest when he coughed. The doctor who had the prank played on him at medical school, let's call him Dr Wingit, was on duty that day and his stethoscope was still blocked! Although John's story suggested that pneumonia was a possibility, Dr Wingit decided this was not the diagnosis because he could not hear the expected breath sounds when he listened with his stethoscope. Nevertheless, he arranged for John to have a chest X-ray and, expecting it to be normal, he decided not to wait for the radiologist's expert opinion.

The X-ray showed shadowing in John's right lung. Dr Wingit always found it difficult when things turned out different from expected. In such situations, he tended to stick to his guns and so he explained away the shadowing on John's X-ray as being the result of an excess of tissues on the chest wall, and he sent John home. Fortunately, John was called back to the hospital for treatment when the radiologist's report came through with a diagnosis of pneumonia.

In chapter 8, we considered how medical diagnosis is based on an approach called Bayesian inference, which involves updating the probability for a given diagnosis as more evidence or information becomes available. This story shows how a diagnostic process based on Bayesian principles can go wrong when an abnormal sensory input (the blocked stethoscope) is combined with a bias against updating hypotheses.

Belief Formation and the Autonomic Nervous System

In the last chapter, we looked how worship activates the autonomic nervous system. In recent years, the study of medical conditions in which the patient wrongly denies the existence of something has pointed to a role for the autonomic nervous system in how we form beliefs.[1] These conditions are known as delusions of negation, and the first known example was reported in 1880 by Jules Cotard, a French psychiatrist working in the Paris suburb of Vanves. He published the medical history of one of his patients, whom he called Mademoiselle X. The extract below is from the first of five articles he wrote on this condition. Cotard describes his patient, assuring us:

> that she does not have any brain, nor nerves, breasts, stomach or intestines; she is left but with the bones of her disorganized body (these are her own expressions). This delusion of negation branches out to the metaphysical ideas that were once for her the object of the most unwavering faith; she does not have a soul, *God doesn't exist*, and nor does the devil.[2]

Unfortunately, patients with this condition generally do not respond to rational persuasion. Mademoiselle X later died of starvation.

Another condition within this group is Capgras syndrome, where the patient believes that someone they love or a person close to them has been replaced by an imposter. Neuropsychologists have found that Bayesian approaches to belief can be useful in understanding these conditions. Rather than being an abnormality of reason, the disordered beliefs are considered to arise from a justifiable inference made to explain abnormal experiences. In the case of delusions, which involve the denial of something, these

1. McKay, "Delusional Inference."
2. Cotard, cited in Dimitriadis, "Painful Analgesia of Cotard's Syndrome," my italics.

experiences are thought to relate to a reduction in the responsiveness of the autonomic nervous system with corresponding effects on heart rate, blood pressure, breathing, and arousal in response to emotional cues. When the responsiveness of this system is reduced for a loved one, the patient experiences no emotional response to the loved one, and from this abnormal data they infer that the loved one must be an imposter. When this occurs for all stimuli, the absence of an emotional response to everything in their environment leads them to infer that they themselves do not exist.

Many researchers think that a second factor is required to explain why false beliefs continue to be upheld in the face of evidence to the contrary. One body of research suggests that this second feature relates to the way the brain deals with inconsistencies between what is expected and what actually happens. The concept is known as error-processing, and normally the brain interprets these discrepancies as a need to update beliefs about the world. However, if error-processing is disturbed, people may tend to see existing beliefs as providing adequate explanations without any need for updating, thereby reinforcing the incorrect belief.

Although Dr Wingit was clearly not suffering from a delusion, there are clear similarities between the way in which his diagnostic thinking went wrong and the Bayesian understanding of Cotard's and Capgras syndromes. Dr Wingit came to an incorrect diagnosis because of an abnormal experience—he could not hear his patient's breath sounds because his stethoscope was blocked. For Cotard's and Capgras syndrome, the abnormal experience results from an impaired autonomic input. Dr Wingit was also reluctant to update his beliefs when presented with new information, similar to patients with Cotard's and Capgras syndromes.

The Science of Religious Unbelief

Much is written about unbelief in the Bible. A well-known example is found in the Gospel of Mark where a man brought his son to Jesus, hoping that he could cure him of the convulsions his son had suffered since childhood. Desperate to believe that Jesus could heal his son, the man cried out, "I believe; help my unbelief!" (Mark 9:24). His statement was both an expression of faith and an admission that his faith was far from perfect. And this odd mixture of faith and doubt is something that many of us experience. But Jesus healed the man's son despite the father's imperfect faith.

The idea that belief is linked to biology can also be found in the Bible. The opening verse of Psalm 42 draws a parallel between the desire for God and the panting of a deer, for example. It is easy to imagine that the deer's panting reflects a deep thirst, but science tells us that deer pant to cool off when they are too hot. Deer have very few sweat glands, and the rapid movement of air through the nasal passages and lungs can reduce their body temperature owing to increased evaporation of water. Behaviors that stabilize body temperature in this way are driven by the autonomic nervous system which, as we have seen, plays an important part in belief formation.

The Bible even hints at a role for impaired sensory inputs in unbelief (John 12:37–41). So perhaps it is possible to use the science of belief formation to construct a biological model for why some people come to deny the existence of God. This model could then point to ways to help unbelief. This idea may seem strange for skeptics, who are more inclined to wonder why some people develop a genuine and active commitment to God. But it is equally valid to ask why some people reject the idea of God. As discussed in chapter 1, considering how different assumptions might affect the interpretation of data is an essential part of the scientific method. Furthermore, as increasingly recognized by psychologists of religion, experience of God is sufficiently widespread as to be regarded as the usual state of affairs, reflecting the functioning of psychological processes that are present in all normal human brains.

In medical science, the study of rare but severe forms of disease can give clues to the basis for less-pronounced but more-common expressions of the same condition. For example, the study of a rare genetic disorder known as familial hypercholesterolemia, in which patients have high levels of cholesterol in their blood, uncovered biological processes that later informed the development of statins, one of the most widely prescribed drugs in modern medicine. In the same way, knowledge of diseases in which someone develops a fixed belief that part of the self, part of the body, or other persons no longer exist may bring to light biological process that can lead healthy to people to deny the existence of God.

Let us start by considering whether reduced autonomic responses combined with a resistance to update beliefs could lie behind religious unbelief. Like Mademoiselle X, patients with Cotard's syndrome can lose previously held religious convictions. And there are other features of atheism that also occur with Cotard's syndrome. For example, Cotard's syndrome is strongly associated with depression, and it is well documented that rates of depression are higher among atheists than among religious people. Moreover, an impairment of face processing has been identified as a key neuropsychological feature of Cotard's and Capgras syndromes. This finding parallels research from the University of Helsinki, Finland, which has demonstrated a reduced ability for religious skeptics to detect face-like features from pictures of scenery and landscapes, and a diminished capacity for evaluating the emotionality of these areas.[3] But this is not to suggest that unbelief in general is a mental disorder. Clearly, most people who deny God's existence do not also deny the existence of their internal body organs! However, unbelief can be understood as a variation in the normal biological processes that would generally lead to belief in God.

Given that people of faith typically liken their interactions with God to an interpersonal relationship, Capgras syndrome may be closer to disbelief in God. In Capgras syndrome, autonomic nervous system responses are reduced in the presence of a loved one, whereas a failure to recognize God would entail a reduction in autonomic responses to stimuli connected to experiences or situations that point to a reality beyond the self, beyond the here and now. These experiences could be considered as an encounter with God, although not necessarily identified as such by the individual concerned. Population studies show that these kinds of experiences are quite common and can be triggered by a range of things, including worship, prayer, the beauty of music or nature, and absorption in creativity. This is not to say that atheists are less appreciative of music or nature, or less likely to be absorbed in creativity, rather that these stimuli may be associated with relatively reduced autonomic responses, leading to an absent or significantly impaired emotional response. From this reduced emotionality, he or she infers that God probably does not exist (at least a God that is loving and good). A disturbance in error processing then creates a bias towards existing beliefs such that this agnosticism tends to become a firm rejection of God.

3. Riekki et al., "Paranormal and Religious Believers."

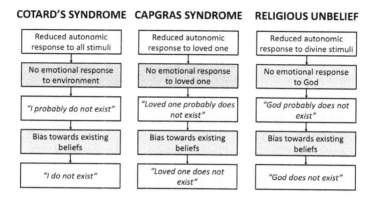

Figure 7: A model for religious unbelief based on the neuropsychology of Cotard's and Capgras syndromes

Is there scientific data to support this Bayesian model for unbelief? There is a significant body of research confirming that emotional responses are relatively reduced among atheists. Examples include a study by Canadian psychologists Christopher Burris and Raluca Petrican which found that atheists show reduced intensity of emotional response to recalled love experiences or tragic news in comparison to religious individuals.[4] In a later study, Burris reported that atheists are more likely to suppress emotional displays than both agnostics and religiously affiliated people, and that restricting the outward display of emotion can amplify beliefs that are consistent with an atheistic worldview.[5] Other studies indicate that atheists are more inclined to base moral choices on the consequences of the action rather than whether that action itself is right or wrong. This approach to moral decisions has also been shown to be associated with reduced emotional arousal.[6]

There is also scientific data that shows differences in how atheists and religious individuals process errors. Researchers at the University of Toronto studied the brain responses of believers and non-believers during a color-naming task that comprised a sequence of individual trials, some of which were designed to promote incorrect answers. Subjects with a greater

---

4. Burris and Petrican, "Hearts Strangely Warmed (and Cooled)."
5. Burris, "Poker-Faced and Godless."
6. Szekely et al., "Religiosity Enhances Emotion."

belief in God not only showed a reduced neurophysiological response to errors but also committed fewer errors.[7]

In a later experiment, participants were exposed to religious concepts immediately before undertaking the task.[8] For believers, both the neurophysiological changes during incorrect responses and the number of mistakes reduced even further, while atheists demonstrated a heightened defensive response to error. In both experiments, the trials promoting errors were in the minority and were therefore relatively unexpected. Accordingly, the data points to a tendency for non-believers to show more intense responses to discrepancies between what is expected and what actually happens, matching the second factor proposed in Bayesian models of mistaken belief.

It may be tempting to argue that the autonomic response to divine stimuli is abnormally increased in people who believe in God rather than being reduced in non-believers. However, with this interpretation, religious belief would not be consistent with the proposed model of disordered belief formation because there is no evidence that a heightened response to prediction errors is present among believers.

Readers who agree with the views expressed in books such as Richard Dawkins' *The God Delusion* might scoff at a scientific model for unbelief. More commonly, science is used to explain belief away. Ever since Sigmund Freud (1856–1939) published his views on religion in the first half of the twentieth century, people of faith have had to confront the allegation that their belief amounts to a mental disorder. A Bayesian understanding of belief formation offers new resources for those who believe in God to respond effectively to such claims. The scientific data that led to the development of Bayesian models for belief was not available to Freud but has been readily accessible to the New Atheists who claim that belief in God can be considered a delusion. Their failure to refer to this body of work is puzzling, given their stated belief in the importance of science. Perhaps this omission reflects the capacity for Bayesian analysis to account for their rejection of God.

---

7. Inzlicht et al., "Neural Markers of Religious Conviction."

8. Inzlicht and Tullett, "Reflecting on God."

Helping Unbelief

The first scientist to propose a solution to religious unbelief was probably the famous French mathematician Blaise Pascal (1623–1662). On 23rd November 1654, between the hours 10:30 and 12:30 at night, Pascal had an intense religious vision while lying in his bed at home in the Marais district of Paris.[9] We know about this vision because he wrote himself a brief note immediately afterwards, beginning with the single word "FIRE." He kept this note sewn into the lining of his jacket and it was discovered only by chance after his death.

Pascal had shown outstanding abilities in science and mathematics from a very young age. By the age of sixteen, he had developed his own theorem on geometry. He went on to lay the groundwork for game theory and to invent the barometer and the syringe, but after his "night of fire," he focused his rational mathematical and scientific mind on the defense of Christianity.

Despite his track record in science, Pascal is particularly well known for emphasizing the importance of intuition and emotion in religious belief. We can see this in the following well-known quotation from his last work, *Pensées* (*Thoughts*): "It is the heart which perceives God and not the reason. This is what faith is: God perceived by the heart, not by the reason."[10]

Pascal's answer to unbelief was remarkable: "You want to be cured of unbelief, and you ask for the remedy. Learn from those who were once bound like you . . . They behaved just as if they did believe, taking holy water, having masses said, and so on. That will make you believe quite naturally."[11] But why should that work? Pascal even pinpointed a key factor underlying how belief in God is gained and maintained: "Proofs only convince the mind. Habit provides the strongest proofs and those that are most believed. It inclines the automaton, which leads the mind unconsciously with it."[12] Pascal uses the word "automaton" to refer to automatic, intuitive mental processes which we now know to be founded on the functions of autonomic nervous system.

Earlier, we saw how a failure of autonomic function can lead to false beliefs. The flip side of this fact is that an active autonomic nervous system

9. Frakenberry, *Faith of Scientists*, 79–101.

10. Pascal, translated by Krailsheimer, *Pensées*, 424.

11. Pascal, translated by Krailsheimer, *Pensées*, 418.

12. Pascal, translated by Krailsheimer, *Pensées*, 821.

can support belief and, as we saw in the last chapter, if done well, public worship can stimulate autonomic responses that are centered on God. These autonomic and emotional responses to God are not in conflict with more rational and reasoned approaches to faith; rather, these two modes are complementary. But, in Pascal's words, "We must make no mistake about ourselves; we are as much automaton as mind."[13]

The Impact of Public Worship on Others

As well as supporting the faith of participants already committed to God, activities of public worship may promote religious belief in others. Contrary to the view that individuals can be convinced by argument alone, a growing body of evidence suggests that people are more likely to believe in God if they witness behaviors that signal to others a genuine belief. (Chapter 3 discussed how changes in behavior can provide a way to validate subjective experiences.) In other words, actions speak louder than words, and actions that trigger the autonomic nervous system may be particularly important. Facial expressions and vocal inflections may signal genuine belief to others, in a similar manner to romantic commitment.

The autonomic nervous system is known to play a key role in these forms of non-verbal communication. The simple act of observing someone else's movements, such as changes in posture during public worship, has also been shown to stimulate autonomic activity. Autonomic functions, such a breathing and heart rate, tend to become synchronized during group singing or speaking. Incorporating into public worship activities that activate the autonomic nervous system may therefore promote religious belief in others as well as sustain the faith of participants already committed to God.

To communicate a commitment to God effectively, the actions concerned need to be regarded as costly to someone not holding the underlying belief. The evolutionary anthropologist Joseph Henrich has called such behaviors "Credibility Enhancing Displays," or CREDs.[14] Relevant actions are not limited to acts of concern for the well-being of others but also include frequent religious attendance and extravagant rituals. A key principle underlying this book maintains that it is justifiable to reinterpret scientific data from a perspective that allows for the existence of God. From this

13. Pascal, translated by Krailsheimer, *Pensées*, 821.

14. Henrich, "Evolution of Costly Displays."

standpoint, CREDs are not seen as encouraging people towards an irrational belief or delusion, but as actions which, when combined with rational thought, lead people towards the reality of God.

In many Western countries, the numbers of people professing belief in God and attendance rates at religious services have both fallen significantly since the Second World War. Any light that science can throw on these circumstances deserves serious consideration by religious communities. Research has shown a link between the number of non-believers in a society and the extent to which people feel that their survival and well-being can be taken for granted. The freer a nation is from threats such as disease, unemployment, and economic inequality, the lower the number of religious participants. Oxford anthropologist Jonathan Lanman has proposed that this connection reflects the effects that threats have on actions. Threatening stimuli lead to an increase in religious actions, which in turn make religious belief more credible to others.[15] The high proportion of non-believers in Denmark and Sweden therefore mirrors the high level of social welfare and reduced threats to the well-being and safety of the population. On the other hand, religious commitment remains high in the USA, where significant sections of society continue to experience distinct threats to well-being and survival as a consequence of weak social welfare policy and economic inequality.

We have already seen how reduced functionality in the autonomic nervous system may lead to religious disbelief. Autonomic reactions are also likely to underlie this connection between threats and religious action. When threatened, animals typically respond with a "fear, flight, or fight" response brought about through the actions of the autonomic nervous system. This response also causes many species of animal to group together (imagine, for example, how sheep flock together when a sheepdog is near). An equivalent response to threats can be observed in humans, but it is seen as increased commitment to and participation in group behaviors, including religious rituals. Conversely, an absence of threats will lead to a reduction in the autonomic responses that promote group behaviors, resulting in lower levels of religious participation. In addition, when threatened, humans tend to adopt faster, intuitive modes of thinking rather than slower, more methodical analytical thought processes.[16] As highlighted in chapter 12, religious disbelief is associated with a bias against intuitive modes of thought and will therefore

15. Lanman, "Importance of Religious Displays."
16. Margittai et al., "Exogenous Cortisol Causes a Shift."

be promoted when threat levels are low, reducing the incentive for participation in religious action even further.

Faced with an increasingly secular society, some religious communities have chosen to adopt less-elaborate patterns of public worship in the hope of making them more accessible to an increasingly skeptical population. Nevertheless, a clear implication of research in this area is that, for the most part, the exact opposite is required. Simplified patterns of worship are less likely to be considered sufficiently costly to someone not holding the underlying belief and so fail to enhance the credibility of religious belief. The more secular the society, the greater the need for CREDs, including more highly developed rituals that provide the autonomic stimuli required to communicate credibility. However, given the reduced tendency for intuitive thinking in societies with low levels of threat, there will also be a need for better, culturally relevant analytical explanations of religious actions. In view of the key role analytical thinking plays in science, approaches that base these explanations on an integration of scientific and religious thinking are well placed to meet this need.

However, elaborate religious displays may not be ideal for every situation. Even within secure societies with few threats to well-being, there may be groups of individuals for whom welfare and safety are endangered. Particular times or events can also create a more widespread feeling of being threatened. Because the perception of threat will have already prompted group behavior and intuitive thinking, religious actions and environments that stimulate the autonomic nervous system further may become counterproductive. Under these circumstances, short and simple religious displays might be more effective in promoting belief.

The eminent British physicist Lord Kelvin (1824–1907) said, "If you think strongly enough you will be forced by science to the belief in God."[17] Despite Kelvin's assertion, no one can *force* themselves to believe, no matter how much evidence they have. But the combined scientific/theological account of unbelief developed above may reduce fearfulness of unbelief in ourselves and others, and inspire us to reflect Jesus's compassion for people suffering unbelief. Furthermore, this understanding may help to overcome unbelief, not only when it coexists with faith but also when there is skepticism. If science and religion are in conflict, the idea that science could lead to belief in God may be met with a degree of suspicion. Does not science deny all things supernatural? Yes, but we can escape this drawback by recognizing

17. Kelvin, "Lord Kelvin on Religion and Science."

that science's exclusion of the supernatural is a simplifying assumption that is open to question. By rejecting this assumption and reinterpreting scientific data from a perspective that allows for the supernatural, we can gain a deeper understanding of how humans relate to God, with the potential to identify more-effective ways to connect with the divine—for example, through informing patterns of worship.

15

Greater Than the Sum of Its Parts

TELEVISION OR FILM DRAMAS about hospital accident and emergency departments are certainly popular. We seem to be attracted to stories about people handling pain and discomfort, tackling crises that could just as easily happen to us. We are also fascinated by the challenges faced by the many different staff members, both at work and in their personal lives.

Medical dramas are often like detective stories where the culprit to be tracked down is not a villain but a mystery illness or a complex injury. In these shows, as in real life, X-rays provide important clues about what is going on. But even though patients are often shown having an X-ray or a scan, we rarely, if ever, see the role of the radiologist. Yet the radiologist is an essential member of the emergency medical team. Medical imaging has developed so rapidly that specially trained experts are needed to interpret the scans and ensure that the correct diagnosis is made. The changes on these scans can be subtle and potentially overlooked or misread by other members of the emergency team.

Ian is a radiologist who is on duty, reporting X-rays and scans from several emergency departments. This is possible because today X-ray images are in a digital format which can be sent electronically to other locations, a practice known as teleradiology. The digital character of the images has other advantages too, not least the opportunity to apply Artificial Intelligence (AI)—that is, computer software programs that perform some of the tasks which normally require human intelligence. Ian has several scans waiting for him to interpret, but the AI software has alerted him to a scan which might show bleeding into the brain. So Ian looks at this case first. The patient is Lillian, a seventy-eight-year-old lady who has fallen in her care home, hitting her head on the furniture. She takes a blood-thinning drug because she has an irregular heartbeat. Taking the drug reduces Lillian's chances of having a stroke, but in the event of a head injury, blood thinners can increase the likelihood of bleeding.

The AI software Ian is using is not a kind of superintelligence that poses a potential threat to humanity but a targeted application developed in accordance with the ethical standards for medical applications of AI as laid down by the medical colleges and other professional bodies. The software is very good at detecting blood on brain scans, occasionally alerting the radiologist to tiny abnormalities that they might otherwise have overlooked. More often, it flags up cases where the computer has detected something other than blood—for example, an appearance that a radiologist would quickly recognize as being caused by movement of the patient's head during the scan. The software is intended to work this way because it is better to be safe than sorry. But in Lillian's case, Ian confirms the presence of blood and telephones the emergency department so that they can start her treatment immediately.

AI software like this often uses something known as a neural network, which is a collection of multiple computer processing units connected together in a particular way; one which loosely imitates the microstructure of the human brain. Like a human brain, the network can be trained to recognize a particular scan appearance by providing examples with and without the condition of interest, along with the final diagnosis. After a time, the network develops the ability to identify the scans that need to be flagged for urgent attention.

The capacity of a neural network to identify bleeding on a brain scan could not be predicted from even perfect knowledge of an individual processing unit, let alone from the behavior of the individual electrons that drive the computer processors. The performance of the system *emerges* from the way several units are connected together and from the context in which they operate, in this case their previous training to identify blood on brain scans. The network is greater than the sum of its parts, and the whole determines the behavior of its parts (sometimes referred to as "downward causation").

The way in which new properties can arise in complex systems made up of multiple interacting units has become a field of scientific study in its own right and is known as emergence. John Holland, a founding father of the complex systems approach, summarizes the features of systems that show emergent behavior as follows: a) the systems comprise interconnected components that follow simple laws, b) the context in which these components operate determines the function of the emergent patterns, and c) the patterns of behavior occurring at higher levels follow new laws, known as "macro-laws," which would not be anticipated from the rules governing lower levels.[1]

It is not just computer systems that show emergence. Emergent behaviors are also common within the natural world. Examples include the hexagonal patterns created by convection cells in fluids and gases, the behavior of ant colonies, and the herding of sheep in the presence of a predator. A particularly spectacular example is the way a large flock of birds in flight all change direction together. The constantly changing patterns formed by the bird's sudden swooping is mesmerizing and surprising at the same time. In many cases, these activities can be modelled using mathematics.

Emergence and Divine Action

Theologian and biochemist Arthur Peacocke has developed an understanding of divine action that is founded on complex systems with emergent properties and downward causation.[2] His insights supplement the openings in the created order that we considered in earlier chapters through which God can interact with his creation without breaking the laws of nature. The entire natural world can be seen as a complex system of interconnected components operating in the context of God. This divine context will determine the behavior of the system, just as the evaluation of brain scans provided the setting that defined the performance of the AI system Ian was using.

On a smaller scale, the features of a complex system with emergent properties may be present in faith communities. A community of God-inspired people can be looked at as a set of interconnected components that follow simple laws, such as, "Love your God and love your neighbor as yourself" (see Matthew 22:37–40). God's presence would provide the context that determines the function of the emergent patterns, which may vary depending on circumstances. For example, a faith community might take up a new initiative to help the disadvantaged or sick. The macro laws would be represented by theological concepts that could not be anticipated from scientific knowledge alone. This model for a faith community mirrors

1. Holland, *Emergence*.
2. Murphy, "Divine Action, Emergence and Scientific Explanation," 255.

the way Christians feel that their connection to Jesus enables the church to make a difference in the world, just as branches must be connected to a vine in order to bear fruit (John 15:5). On the other hand, skepticism and unbelief may constrain the capacity for God to act (Matthew 13:58; Mark 6:5–6). Although not essential for God to act, a community of faith can facilitate divine action.

Worship services can help to create the conditions that promote emergence within the complex system represented by a faith community. By regularly coming together in one place, the connections between members of the congregation are strengthened. Certain worship actions that synchronize the physiology of the participants, such as group singing, are particularly likely to enhance the cohesion of the group. Worship services also provide an opportunity to reinforce the simple laws that underlie the system and limit the unbelief which can constrain the opportunities for divine action. The overarching narrative of the worship service can consolidate the God-centered context which determines the properties of the emergent patterns. As seen for Artificial Intelligence networks, the performance of the system is like to improve with repeated use.

This model of divine action in which God acts through downward causation in complex systems can also provide a deeper understanding of prayer. Prayer is central to the personal connection to God experienced by people of faith. It is how we communicate with God and he with us. Earlier, we considered how using reason in prayer can show that the words we say to God are reliable and trustworthy (chapter 8), and that God's action on our brains might explain how we can sense God speaking to us (chapter 11). Prayers can take many forms, but often they involve asking God a for specific outcome, either for oneself or on behalf of others. It is possible to see these prayers as just a way to express a longing for a world that is more open to God's influence. But in the main, it is expected that prayers of this sort can also make a difference in the world, and for this to happen, prayer needs to be linked to divine action.

Yet research trials have failed to show any benefit from intercessory prayer where people pray for others who are some distance away. By way of example, let us consider a large study sponsored by the Templeton Foundation, which supports research at the interface of science and religion. This study found that intercessory prayer at a distance had no effect on the recovery of patients undergoing heart bypass surgery. In fact, patients did slightly worse when they knew for certain that people were praying for them.[3]

Trials of prayer of this sort assume that prayer works by prompting God to act when he might otherwise not do so. One implication of this model of prayer is that God may withhold healing someone merely because not enough people have asked him to do it. On the other hand, if healing someone were God's will, surely he would do it regardless of whether anyone had prayed for that outcome. But what if praying for someone were more about changing the person praying than persuading God? Prayer can be seen as a way to align ourselves more closely with the will of God (in accordance with the line from the Lord's Prayer, "Thy will be done"), and this could enhance our ability to function more effectively as an interconnected part of a complex system that facilitates God's action.

Praying for someone in particular can therefore be seen as facilitating God's action in the world in a general way. For a randomized controlled trial of prayer at a distance, this would mean that people in either group could benefit, or even someone not in the trial at all. In this case, the study design would be unable to demonstrate the effects of prayer. So perhaps research should be looking for other more general effects of prayer, such as church growth, which preliminary data suggests is associated with strong prayer practice among faith communities in Korea.[4]

To the scientifically minded, the miracles of Jesus might seem far-fetched. But in a purely scientific statement, John Holland wrote, "Transformation from the extremely unlikely to the likely is a major characteristic of systems exhibiting emergent phenomena."[5] When we have a complex system, whose behavior is shaped by God, we should expect the seemingly improbable to happen; unlikely events that some might even describe as "miraculous."

3. Benson et al., "Study of the Therapeutic Effects."
4. Kang, "Prayer and Church Growth."
5. Holland, *Emergence*, 231.

— 16 —

Online Worship

BRIAN HAS DEVELOPED A red rash on his nose and cheeks. He also has spots on his nose. Although in his early sixties, the rash reminds Brian of when he was a teenager—it looks a bit like acne. Hoping there might be a cream that will clear his rash up, Brian decides to get advice from his doctor but, as the coronavirus pandemic is underway, he has to have his consultation online. Brian is fine with the idea of an online consultation. It can hardly be harder than ordering his groceries, which he has been doing online since the start of the pandemic.

He loads the appropriate web page and, after answering written questions that check that he is not having a heart attack or other emergency, Brian fills in his personal details and indicates the nature of his problem. After a few more questions, the screen suddenly fills with twenty or more color pictures of noses, each with a different kind of rash. Brian is asked to choose the one that looks closest to his own nose. He feels a little uncomfortable but is also relieved that his rash is not on a more embarrassing part of his body. As he studies the pictures more closely, he sees one that reminds him of Jack, who runs the local newsagent's. He makes a mental note to look more closely at Jack's nose next time he sees him, but then remembers that Jack will probably be wearing a mask.

Brian chooses a nose that is like his own and answers a few more written questions. The process ends with a note saying the surgery will contact him in the next twenty-four hours. The next day, he receives an email from the surgery saying that the doctor has prescribed a cream which he can pick up from the pharmacy in a couple of days. Although Brian has received the treatment he needed, he missed the in-person interaction with a health care professional. "You will never get the same experience with an online consultation," he thinks.

Of course, medical care was not the only activity to move online during the coronavirus pandemic. During 2020 and 2021, many countries closed churches as part of the measures to curb the spread of infection, and there was also a corresponding increase in participation in online worship. Online services of worship, live or recorded, represented one way in which faith communities could maintain their pursuits in the face of the world health crisis. Often streamed from a church leader's home, these services proved to be very popular. On Palm Sunday 2020, one Church of England service was watched by more than 400,000 people.

Online worship was not new at the time of the pandemic. Christian communities have existed online since the 1980s. Some Christian commentators have expressed concerns that the participants in online worship are inevitably disconnected from their physical being. In many cases, the congregation may largely be entirely passive observers. Yet, as we have seen in earlier chapters, worship involves much more than an expression of a set of beliefs through words alone. Postures and actions adopted during worship are also an essential part of spiritual experience, often triggering a large array of associated feelings, thoughts, and actions. Yet including these physical aspects of worship have presented a significant challenge for online churches. This problem may have mattered less in the past because the majority of participants also worshipped "offline."[1] But during the pandemic, it was not possible to make up for any limitations of online services by combining them with local church attendance.

Much has been written about online worship during the pandemic, both academic papers and popular books. In general, the reactions reported in these publications mirror Brian's thoughts about online medicine—the experience is simply not the same as attending church in person. Yet we should remember that most online services were either prerecorded or streamed live, and these formats may constrain the implementation of some of the aspects of worship discussed in earlier chapters. Other online environments, such as teleconferencing software (e.g., Zoom) or virtual reality, might be more effective. Therefore, we should not discount online worship altogether. For some Christians, this may be their preferred choice, perhaps after experiencing online worship for the first time during the pandemic. For others, online worship may be the only option.

---

1. Hutchings, "Dis/Embodied Church," 43.

Furthermore, some people will review a church's online content before deciding whether to attend in person.

We can use the science of worship outlined in earlier chapters to identify the strengths and weaknesses of online worship, and to identify opportunities for optimizing the online experience. The experience may also underscore the importance of some aspects of worship that we might have begun to take for granted, and point to ways in which in-person worship might also be improved.

In previous chapters, we have seen that specific ways in which words are spoken and the bodily postures and actions undertaken during worship are not arbitrary customs adopted only for their symbolic meaning. They can bring about a range of beneficial outcomes, as summarized below:

Thoughts and Beliefs

- Narratives enacted in communal worship greatly influence attitudes and behaviors.

- Worshippers are more open to religious narratives when the speaker is regarded as having influential authority and/or when the narratives are accompanied by rituals.

- Linking religious ideas to specific gestures and body positions can make abstract concepts easier to understand and remember.

- Saying words in specific ways and participating in worship actions can support belief in God.

Health Benefits

- Physical activities that form part of worship contribute to better physical health.

- Postures and movements can affect thoughts and emotions in ways that boost mental health.

Openness to God

- Worship services can bring about conditions that facilitate God's cooperative action with individuals and communities of faith.

Signaling Belief to Others

- Worship actions can lead others to a life of faith by signaling a genuine commitment to God.

To what extent can these benefits be achieved online? Many of the worship behaviors reviewed in earlier chapters are just as feasible online as offline. But there are some worship activities that would be difficult or impossible to implement, particularly with prerecorded or streamed worship. For example, bodily reactions triggered by the smell of burning incense or the taste of communion wine would be difficult to recreate fully, although the effects of incense could possibly be simulated by using a scented candle at home. (Many Christian dominations do not allow online participants to make a substitution for communion wine.) The physiological effects of joint singing or speaking may be achievable online. However, recalling the research that showed differences in the state of the brain when speaking in unison with a live voice as compared to prerecorded speech, the full effects of joint singing and speaking may only be achievable when interactive online worship environments are used. Research also suggests that the physiological impact of a given posture may depend on whether the participant is being observed. The effects of worship postures may therefore be different for online services that use video streaming as opposed to videoconferencing software.

A significant limitation for online worship is the reduced capacity for non-verbal communication of belief to others by means of bodily postures and movements. Even with interactive online environments such as conferencing software, worshippers may not be able to appreciate fully the actions and postures of other participants, unless they are using software that allows their camera to track movements. The fact that online worshippers typically do not leave their homes will also reduce the visibility of religious behaviors within their communities. Even the simple fact that a group of people forgoing the pursuit of leisure can be seen travelling to a place of worship, perhaps in response to church bells, provides a visible signal of commitment to God. As considered in chapter 14, research suggests that a lack of exposure to religious actions is an important factor in unbelief. It would be unfortunate if an expansion of online worship were to make these circumstances worse, albeit inadvertently.

On the other hand, online environments can potentially enhance worship in ways that may not be possible in real-life places of worship. Much of the research data highlighted in earlier chapters was acquired using computers, and the implications of this research can be readily applied to some forms of online worship. For example, online worship can make the most of the demonstrable relationship between God-related concepts and position in space by using captions located at the top of the screen (i.e., surtitles rather than subtitles). In addition, the physiological changes associated with the orienting responses could be triggered by intermittently superimposing visual targets, perhaps images of religious objects or symbols, in the upper part of the screen.

In his book *Visiting Online Church: A Journey Exploring Effective Digital Christian Community*, Peter DeHaan includes a valuable compilation of reactions from people who had participated in online church during the coronavirus pandemic.[2] Some comments highlighted the importance of in-person interactions during worship, something that was lost with online church. "I miss being inspired and encouraged by the worship of others," was one response, while another complained, "You cannot make eye contact."

DeHaan's book also brings to light a practical difficulty with online worship that at first glance might not be expected. Many online participants expressed a reluctance to join in with worship actions. Approximately one-third of participants found it hard to sing along when at home. "I try to sing along but find it uncomfortable," and, "I feel my meager attempts to sing distract from their pure and engaging worship," are examples of individual responses. Some worship leaders were clearly aware of this problem and encouraged the congregation to sing along with them, "even if it feels awkward."[3]

Encouraging particular postures, such as kneeling or standing, should also be straightforward online—for example, by verbal or text prompts. Seeing the worship leader adopt a particular posture could also provide a helpful cue to participants. Even observing another's actions

2. DeHaan, *Visiting Online Church*.
3. DeHaan, *Visiting Online Church*, 105.

is known to induce changes in physiology. Interestingly, the coronavirus pandemic resulted in large numbers of people taking part in live-streamed fitness workouts. Clearly, it is possible to encourage people to join in with group actions in an online environment. However, this seems to be harder to achieve for worship actions.

Why should performing worship actions online be problematic for some people? Again, clues can be found in DeHaan's book, which highlights how pre-existing attitudes towards the online environment can affect the worship experience. One contributor says online worship "feels just like the countless Zoom meetings I do at work," while another tells us, "It feels like I'm watching a show rather than participating in a service." DeHaan's own reflections on prerecorded custom content created for an online experience and livestream worship services show how each format can bring its own differing expectations. He compares custom content to the informal, personal videos found on social media but likens livestream worship to a television production.[4]

In chapter 12, we considered how the words and actions performed during worship enact an overarching Christian narrative that influences the thoughts and actions of the participants. With regular participation, simply entering a place of worship will trigger the attitudes and behaviors associated with the worship narrative. James K. A. Smith highlights how other regular activities of everyday life also carry narratives of a non-religious kind and, just like worship, these narratives affect our attitudes and behaviors.[5] When transferring worship to fresh surroundings, we may encounter previously learnt narratives associated with the new environment. For example, a shopping mall will carry with it attitudes and behaviors centered on commercial transactions. These alternative narratives may be incompatible with the narrative intended from the worship activities. The same principle will apply to online environments. If we have become accustomed to using computers for activities other than worship, the online environment will come with attitudes and behaviors that we have already learnt, and these may not be conducive to singing or performing bodily actions and postures.

One aspect of the online environment that could conflict with Christian worship is summed up by the notion of disembodiment. This term refers to the way that digital media tend to disconnect selves from bodies. In

4. DeHaan, *Visiting Online Church*, 176.
5. Smith, *Imagining the Kingdom*.

a digital environment, the body is no longer fully required, and the user can participate in online activities independently from their body. For some people, the disembodiment experienced online may resonate with particular ideas about religion, especially the view that the goal of spirituality is to escape the physical body and the material world in order to pass into a realm of pure spirit where one can be free and content. This perspective is much closer to a philosophy known as Gnosticism than it is to Christianity, which sees the material world as essentially good but flawed, and upholds the concept of a future bodily existence in a new creation. Given the tendency for digital environments to foster disembodiment, an emphasis on bodily postures and actions may be even more important for online worship than for in-person church services.

Is online worship here to stay, even though the end of the coronavirus pandemic is within sight? In 2021, a partnership between Infinity Concepts and Grey Matter Research surveyed more than a thousand American Protestants to explore their experiences with temporary substitutes for in-person worship during the pandemic.[6] Although most of those who participated in online worship considered in-person services to provide a better experience, only 44 percent expressed a preference to return exclusively to in-person worship. The majority wished to include online services as part of their ongoing worship practice, with 2 percent intending to worship exclusively online. It is therefore likely that setting up online worship during the pandemic will change worship in the long term.

Science frequently underpinned the responses of governments around the world to the coronavirus pandemic. When combined with Christian thinking, science can also help to promote the effectiveness of online worship into the future.

---

6. Grey Matter Research and Infinity Concepts, *Ripple Effect*.

17

Science as an Act of Worship

IF YOU WERE A scientist with a strong commitment to God, would you consider being ordained as a priest? Many have. John Polkinghorne is a notable example, but when the seventeenth-century scientist and theologian Robert Boyle was encouraged to do so, he declined. British historian of science John Hedley Brooke sums up Boyle's reasons nicely:

> His defense of Christianity and of its harmony with science would be more effective if he remained a layman. To write as a clergyman would have risked the cynical retort that "He would say that wouldn't he?" Boyle was content, in his own words to be a "priest in the temple of nature."[1]

The main purpose of exploring the science of worship in this book is to offer a fresh explanation of church. But it is also possible to see the science presented as contributing to the priestly role envisaged by Boyle. For Boyle, all of creation provides evidence of God's glory, but only humans have the ability to gather and organize that evidence and put it into words that return thanks and praises to the Creator, which they do not only for themselves but also for the whole creation. From this perspective, rather than being irreligious, the study of the natural world becomes a duty to God which makes full use of the gift of reason. Boyle's proposition can be grounded on the network of experiences and theories that constitute Christian thinking, in particular a full understanding of the impact of the Crucifixion and Resurrection of Jesus. Through the cross, not just humanity but also the whole of creation will be brought into perfect integration with God (Colossians 1:20).

1. Brooke, "Legacy of Robert Boyle," 116.

The fact that God took on human nature (as Jesus) to achieve this outcome points to a responsibility towards the natural world that humanity was meant to fulfil but had failed to accomplish. As bearers of God's image, humankind has a duty to act as a bridge between God and his creation, reflecting God into the natural world and offering up the natural world to God for blessing. Because of the similarities with the way priests mediate between God and the people, these tasks are sometimes described as a calling to be "priests of creation," which is one way in which to take part in the process by which God will, in the end, make all things right (see chapter 12).

Boyle suggested that science can contribute to worship in much the same way as musical instruments do: "And on the opened body of the same animal, a skillful anatomist will make reflections, as much more to the honour of its Creator . . . As the musick made on a lute by a rare lutanist."[2] And some of the reasons that are given for including musical instruments in worship also apply to science. Both are ways of including the natural world in worship in much the same way as bread and wine are used in the Eucharist and water in Baptism. Science is not just about analysis; it is also about creativity in much the same way that playing a musical instrument is creative, in that scientists have to use their imaginations to come up with explanations and solutions. The playing of musical instruments and the inclusion of science in worship can therefore help us to more deeply express our God-given creativity. Both musical instruments and science can also make our worship more culturally relevant.

There is a minority of Christians who hold that musical instruments should not be used for worship. They argue that the Old Testament temple with its use of instruments has given way to the "living temple" of the human body (1 Corinthians 6:19), for which only the living, spirit-filled instrument of the human voice is appropriate. The idea that knowledge of human neuroscience and physiology can enhance worship fits with this view just as well if not better. These sciences are wholly appropriate to worship within the living temple of the human body, where greater awareness of how the human body works should help people of faith to "present [their] bodies as a living sacrifice" (Romans 12:1).

When drawing a parallel between science and musical instruments as ways to enhance worship, Boyle specifically references the science of anatomy. Today, X-rays and other medical imaging techniques are increasingly used to demonstrate anatomy, either in conjunction with or

2. Boyle, cited in Fisch, "Scientist as Priest," 259.

in place of dissection. Given the way this book has drawn on medical imaging to illustrate the science of worship, perhaps it is permissible to paraphrase Boyle in a more modern context by suggesting that a skillful radiologist may make reflections on the images of the internal structure and function of the human body that are as much to the honor of its creator as the music made on a church organ by an outstanding organist, or the guitars and drums of an exceptional worship band. Exploring the scientific aspects of worship within a context of Christian faith can be both a response to God and a way to be shaped by him. Engaging science for worship can itself be an act of worship.

Boyle is not the only thinker to regard the study of the natural world as a priestly role. More recently, the Scottish Theologian Thomas F. Torrance (1913–2007) has written:

> Man as scientist can be spoken of as the priest of creation, whose office it is to interpret the books of nature written by the finger of God, to unravel the universe in its marvelous patterns and symmetries, and to bring it all into orderly articulation in such a way that it fulfills its proper end as the vast theater of glory in which the Creator is worshipped and hymned and praised by his creatures.[3]

But can the science of worship be a part of this vision? No doubt, there are potential pitfalls. One possible concern is that the scientific study of religious interactions is in itself corrosive to faith in a way that does not apply to, say, the study of electrons or the human eye.[4] Unlike many areas of science, the scientific study of religion had its origins in the emerging atheism of the late seventeenth and early eighteenth centuries. But since the mid twentieth century, more and more people of faith have participated in this field of study, stimulated by the establishment of research departments within church-affiliated colleges and universities and the formation of new denominational organizations directed towards the research of religion. These developments affirm the view that the biological and sociological aspects of religion can be studied scientifically without eliminating the supernatural.

Another concern is that the scientific study of religion may separate worship from the vision of God. C. S. Lewis warns of this danger in his *Reflections on the Psalms*, where he writes:

3. Torrance, *Ground and Grammar of Theology*, 5–6.
4. Stark, "Atheism, Faith."

No sooner is it possible to distinguish the rite from the vision of God than there is a danger of the rite becoming a substitute for, and a rival to, God Himself. Once it can be thought of separately, it will; and it may then take on a rebellious, cancerous life of its own.[5]

Within the Psalms, Lewis identifies a way to avert this danger, and it is one that we can also apply to scientific explanations of worship. We must remember that understanding what happens during worship is not the real point at all. God doesn't need our explanations of worship any more than he needs burnt offerings. But rather than convert worship into a science, it is possible for science to become a vehicle for praising God, just as human life became the vehicle of divine life in the person of Jesus.

5. Lewis, *Reflections on the Psalms*, 38.

Bibliography

Armstrong, Karen. *Fields of Blood: Religion and the History of Violence.* London: Random, 2015.

———. *The Case for God: What Religion Really Means.* London: Random, 2009.

Augustine. *The Literal Meaning of Genesis.* Vol. 1, *Books 1–6.* Edited by Johannes Quasten et al. Translated and annotated by John Hammond Taylor et al. Ancient Christian Writers. New York: Newman, 1982.

Barna Group. "How Different Generations View and Engage with Charismatic and Pentecostal Christianity." March 29, 2010. www.barna.com/research/how-different-generations-view-and-engage-with-charismatic-and-pentecostal-christianity.

Barnes, M. Elizabeth, et al. "Are Scientists Biased Against Christians? Exploring Real and Perceived Bias Against Christians in Academic Biology." *PloS one* 15 (2020) e0226826.

Batson, C. Daniel. "Individual Religion, Tolerance, and Universal Compassion." In *Religion, Intolerance, and Conflict: A Scientific and Conceptual Investigation.*, edited by Steve Clarke, Russell Powell, and Julian Savulescu, 88–106. Oxford: Oxford University Press, 2013.

Bennett Bean, William, ed. *Sir William Osler: Aphorisms from his Bedside Teachings collected by Robert Bennett Bean.* New York: Henry Schuman, 1950.

Benson, Herbert, et al. "Study of the Therapeutic Effects of Intercessory Prayer (STEP) in Cardiac Bypass Patients: A Multicenter Randomized Trial of Uncertainty and Certainty of Receiving Intercessory Prayer." *American Heart Journal* 151 (2006) 934–42.

Bernardi, Luciano, et al. "Effect of Rosary Prayer and Yoga Mantras on Autonomic Cardiovascular Rhythms: Comparative Study." *BMJ* 323 (2001) 1446–49.

Born, Max. *The Born-Einstein Letters with Commentaries by Max Born.* Translated by I. Born. London: Macmillan, 1971.

Brierley, Justin. *Unbelievable? Why After Ten Years of Talking with Atheists, I'm Still a Christian.* London: SPCK, 2017.

Brooke, John Hedley. "The Legacy of Robert Boyle: Then and Now." In *Science and Religion in the Twenty-First Century*, edited by Russell Re Manning and Michael Byrne, 114–28. Norwich: SCM, 2013.

Brown, C. Mackenzie. "The Conflict Between Religion and Science in Light of the Patterns of Religious Belief Among Scientists." *Zygon* 38 (2003) 603–32.

Burris, Christopher T. "Poker-Faced and Godless: Expressive Suppression and Atheism." *Psychology of Religion and Spirituality* 14 (2022) 351–61.

Burris, Christopher T., and Raluca Petrican. "Hearts Strangely Warmed (and Cooled): Emotional Experience in Religious and Atheistic Individuals." *International Journal for the Psychology of Religion* 21 (2011) 183–97.

Carrazana, Enrique, and Jocelyn Cheng. "St Theresa's Dart and a Case of Religious Ecstatic Epilepsy." *Cognitive and Behavioral Neurology* 24 (2011) 152–55.

Carrel, Alexis. Cited in "Famous Maxims." https://emedsa.org.au/Students/Maxims.htm.

Chasteen, Alison L., et al. "Thinking of God Moves Attention." *Neuropsychologia* 48 (2010) 627–30.

Chen, Meng, et al. "Persuasive Effects of Linguistic Agency Assignments and Point of View in Narrative Health Messages About Colon Cancer." *Journal of Health Communication* 20 (2015) 977–88.

The Church of England. "Prayer and Worship Resources: B Penitence." www.churchofengland.org/prayer-and-worship/worship-texts-and-resources/common-worship/common-material/new-patterns-12.

Crisp, Thomas M. "An Evolutionary Objection to the Argument from Evil." In *Evidence and Religious Belief*, edited by Kelly James Clark and Raymond J. VanArragon, 114–32. Oxford: Oxford University Press, 2011.

Critchley, Hugo D., et al. "Interaction Between Cognition, Emotion, and the Autonomic Nervous System." *Handbook of Clinical Neurology* 117 (2013) 59–77.

Darwin, Charles. "To William Graham 3 July 1881." Darwin Correspondence Project, University of Cambridge. https://www.darwinproject.ac.uk/letter/DCP-LETT-13230.xml.

Davies, Paul. *God and the New Physics*. New York: Simon & Schuster, 1984.

Dawkins, Richard. *The God Delusion*. London: Bantam, 2006.

———. Speech at the Edinburgh International Science Festival, April 15, 1992, cited in "EDITORIAL: A Scientist's Case against God." *The Independent*, April 20, 1992.

DeHaan, Peter. *Visiting Online Church: A Journey Exploring Effective Digital Christian Community*. Grand Rapids: Rock Rooster, 2021.

Dicks, Terrance. *The Eight Doctors*. London: BBC, 1997.

Dimitriadis, Yorgos. "The Painful Analgesia of Cotard's Syndrome." *The Open Pain Journal* 7 (2014) 36–40.

Einstein, Albert. *Ideas and Opinions*. New York: Wings, 1954.

Fehige, Yiftach. "The Book of Job as a Thought Experiment: On Science, Religion, and Literature." *Religions* 10 (2019) 77.

Feinberg, Joel. *The Moral Limits of the Criminal Law*. Vol. 1, *Harm to Others*. Oxford: Oxford University Press, 1984.

Fisch, Harold. "The Scientist as Priest: A Note on Robert Boyle's Natural Theology." *Isis* 44 (1953) 252–65.

Frankenberry, Nancy K., ed. *The Faith of Scientists: In Their Own Words*. Princeton: Princeton University Press, 2008.

Freeburg, Paige A., et al. "Meaning Behind the Movement: Attributing Sacred Meaning to Fluid and Nonfluid Arm Movements Increases Self-Transcendent Positive Emotions and Buffers the Effects of Nonfluidity on Positive Emotions." *Psychology of Religion and Spirituality* (2022).

Gervais, Will M., and Ara Norenzayan. "Analytic Thinking Promotes Religious Disbelief." *Science* 336 (2012) 493–96.

Gomes, Marleide da Mota, and R. Brian Haynes. "William Osler (1849–1919) at the Roots of Evidence-Based Medicine." *Canadian Journal of General Internal Medicine* 14 (2019) 23–27.

Grayling, A. C. *The God Argument: The Case Against Religion and for Humanism.* London: A. & C. Black, 2013.

Greene, Joshua D., et al. "The Neural Bases of Cognitive Conflict and Control in Moral Judgment." *Neuron* 44 (2004) 389–400.

Grey Matter Research and Infinity Concepts. *The Ripple Effect: Congregations, COVID, and the Future of Church Life,* 2021.

Gross, Neil, and Solon Simmons. "The Religiosity of American College and University Professors." *Sociology of Religion* 70 (2009) 101–29.

Gunderman, Richard B., and Benjamin A. Tritle. "First-Generation Radiography: The Patient's Perspective." *Radiology* 259 (2011) 321–23.

Hameroff, Stuart R., et al. "Quantum Effects in the Understanding of Consciousness." *Journal of Integrative Neuroscience* 13 (2014) 229–52.

Harari, Yuval Noah. *Homo Deus: A Brief History of Tomorrow.* London: Random, 2016.

Harris, Sam, et al. "The Neural Correlates of Religious and Nonreligious Belief." *PLoS one* 4 (2009) e7272.

Henrich, Joseph. "The Evolution of Costly Displays, Cooperation and Religion: Credibility Enhancing Displays and Their Implications for Cultural Evolution." *Evolution and Human Behavior* 30 (2009) 244–60.

Hill, Austin Bradford. "The Environment and Disease: Association or Causation?" *Proceedings of the Royal Society of Medicine* 58 (1965) 295–300.

Hitchens, Christopher. *God Is Not Great: How Religion Poisons Everything.* Toronto: McClelland & Stewart, 2008.

Holland, John H. *Emergence: From Chaos to Order.* Oxford: Oxford University Press, 2000.

Hruska, Pam, et al. "Hemispheric Activation Differences in Novice and Expert Clinicians During Clinical Decision Making." *Advances in Health Sciences Education* 21 (2016) 921–33.

Hutchings, David, and Tom McLeish. *Let There Be Science: Why God Loves Science, and Science Needs God.* Oxford: Lion, 2017.

Hutchings, Tim. "The Dis/Embodied Church: Worship, New Media and the Body." In *Christianity in the Modern World: Changes and Controversies,* edited by Elijah Obinna et al., 49–70. Abingdon: Routledge, 2016.

Huxley, Aldous. *Ends and Means: An Inquiry into the Nature of Ideals and into the Methods Employed for their Realization.* Transaction, 1937.

Ide, George H. "The X-Rays." *Homiletic Review* NS 31 (1866) 514–18.

Inzlicht, Michael, et al. "Neural Markers of Religious Conviction." *Psychological Science* 20 (2009) 385–92.

Inzlicht, Michael, and Alexa M. Tullett. "Reflecting on God: Religious Primes Can Reduce Neurophysiological Response to Errors." *Psychological Science* 21 (2010) 1184–90.

Jasmin, Kyle M., et al. "Cohesion and Joint Speech: Right Hemisphere Contributions to Synchronized Vocal Production." *Journal of Neuroscience* 36 (2016) 4669–80.

Kang, Seung I. "Prayer and Church Growth in the Korean Church." PhD thesis, 2000.

Kark, J. D., et al. "Does Religious Observance Promote Health? Mortality in Secular vs Religious Kibbutzim in Israel." *American Journal of Public Health* 86 (1996) 341–46.

Kelly, Thomas. "*Consensus Gentium*: Reflections on the 'Common Consent' Argument for the Existence of God." In *Evidence and Religious Belief*, edited by Kelly James Clark and Raymond J. VanArragon, 135–56. Oxford: Oxford University Press, 2011.

Kelvin, Lord. "Lord Kelvin on Religion and Science." zapatopi.net/kelvin/papers/science_affirms_creative_power.html.

Kishimoto, Yasuzumi et al. "Reossification of Osteolytic Metastases at the Acetabulum Following Gefitinib and Multidisciplinary Ttreatment for Lung Cancer: A Case Report with Autopsy Findings." *Journal of Orthopaedic Science* 20 (2015) 914–18.

Kondoh, S., et al. "Experiencing Respect Elongates the Orienting Response." 2020.

Krause, Neal, and Christopher G. Ellison. "The Doubting Process: A Longitudinal Study of the Precipitants and Consequences of Religious Doubt in Older Adults." *Journal for the Scientific Study of Religion* 48 (2009) 293–312.

Lambeth Conference Conversations, "Talking About Faith and Science." www.lambethconference.org/resources/talking-about-faith-and-science/#v.

Lamott, Anne. *Bird by Bird: Some Instructions on Writing and Life*. New York: Random, 1994.

Lanman, Jonathan A. "The Importance of Religious Displays for Belief Acquisition and Secularization." *Journal of Contemporary Religion* 27 (2012) 49–65.

Larson, Edward J., and Larry Witham. "Scientists Are Still Keeping the Faith." *Nature* 386 (1997) 435–36.

Lennox, John C. *2084: Artificial Intelligence and the Future of Humanity*. Grand Rapids: Zondervan, 2020.

———. *God's Undertaker: Has Science Buried God?* Oxford: Lion, 2009.

Lentle, Brian, and John Aldrich. "Radiological Sciences, Past and Present." *The Lancet* 350 (1997) 280–85.

Lewis, C. S. *Miracles: A Preliminary Study*. San Francisco: HarperOne, 2001.

———. *Reflections on the Psalms*. Boston: Houghton Mifflin Harcourt, 1958.

———. *The Silver Chair*. The Chronicles of Narnia 6. London: HarperCollins, 2009.

Lupton, Deborah. "Revolting Bodies: The Pedagogy of Disgust in Public Health Campaigns." Department of Sociology and Social Policy, University of Sydney (2013).

Margittai, Zsofia, et al. "Exogenous Cortisol Causes a Shift from Deliberative to Intuitive Thinking." *Psychoneuroendocrinology* 64 (2016) 131–35.

McCormick, Matthew S. "Why Are All of the Gods Hiding?" In *Atheism and the Case Against Christ*, by Matthew S. McCormick, 161–74. New York: Prometheus, 2012.

McCullough, M. E., et al. "Religious Involvement and Mortality: A Meta-analytic Review." *Health Psychology* 19 (2000) 211.

McGrath Alister. *Enriching Our Vision of Reality: Theology and the Natural Sciences in Dialogue*. London: SPCK, 2016.

McKay, Ryan. "Delusional Inference." *Mind & Language* 27 (2012) 330–55.

McLachlan, John C., et al. "Teaching Anatomy Without Cadavers." *Medical Education* 38 (2004) 418–24.

McLeish, Tom. *Faith and Wisdom in Science*. Oxford: Oxford University Press, 2014.

McPherson, David. "Re-Enchanting the World: An Examination of Ethics, Religion, and Their Relationship in the Work of Charles Taylor." Dissertations (2009 -). Paper 280 (2013). http://epublications.marquette.edu/dissertations_mu/280

Meagher, Benjamin R. "Deciphering the Religious Orientation of a Sacred Space: Disparate Impressions of Worship Settings by Congregants and External Observers." *Journal of Environmental Psychology* 55 (2018) 70–80.

Mercier, Hugo, and Dan Sperber. *The Enigma of Reason: A New Theory of Human Understanding.* Cambridge, MA: Harvard University Press, 2017.

Meier, Brian P., et al. "God Is Up? Replication and Extension Attempts of Meier et al. (2007)." *Psychology of Religion and Spirituality* (2021).

Meier, Brian P., et al. "What's 'Up' with God? Vertical Space as a Representation of the Divine." *Journal of Personality and Social Psychology* 93 (2007) 699–710.

Murphy, Nancey. "Divine Action, Emergence, and Scientific Explanation." In *The Cambridge Companion to Science and Religion,* edited by Peter Harrison, 244–59. Cambridge: Cambridge University Press, 2010.

———. "Divine Action in the Natural Order: Buridan's Ass and Schrödinger's Cat." In *Chaos and Complexity: Scientific Perspectives on Divine Action,* by Robert J. Russell, et al., 325–58. Rome: The Vatican Observatory, 1996.

———. "What Has Theology to Learn from Scientific Methodology?" In *Science and Theology: Questions at the Interface,* edited by Murray Rae, et al., 101–26. Edinburgh: T. & T. Clark, 1994.

Neilan, Barbara A. "The Miraculous Cure of a Sarcoma of the Pelvis: Cure of Vittorio Micheli at Lourdes." *The Linacre Quarterly* 80 (2013) 277–81.

Newberg, Andrew B. *Principles of Neurotheology.* Farnham: Ashgate, 2010.

Newberg, Andrew B., et al. "The Measurement of Regional Cerebral Blood Flow During Glossolalia: A Preliminary SPECT Study." *Psychiatry Research: Neuroimaging* 148 (2006) 67–71.

Norenzayan, Ara, and Will M. Gervais. "The Origins of Religious Disbelief." *Trends in Cognitive Sciences* 17 (2013) 20–25.

Oman, Doug, ed. *Why Religion and Spirituality Matter for Public Health.* Vol. 2, *Evidence, Implications, and Resources.* Cham: Springer, 2018.

Pascal, Blaise. *Pensées.* Translated by A. J. Krailsheimer. London: Penguin Classics, 1995.

Payne, Misty M. "Charles Theodore Dotter: The Father of Intervention." *Texas Heart Institute Journal* 28 (2001) 28–38.

Polkinghorne, John. "Where Is Natural Theology Today?" *Science and Christian Belief* 18 (2006) 169–79.

Radhakrishna, R. K. A., et al. "Nonlinear Measures of Heart Rate Time Series: Influence of Posture and Controlled Breathing." *Autonomic Neuroscience* 83 (2000) 148–58.

Ramachandran, V. S. *The Tell-Tale Brain: A Neuroscientist's Quest for What Makes Us Human.* New York: Norton, 2012.

Reeves, Roy R., et al. "Temporal Lobe Discharges and Glossolalia." *Neurocase* 20 (2014) 236–40.

Riekki, Tapani, et al. "Paranormal and Religious Believers Are More Prone to Illusory Face Perception than Skeptics and Non-believers." *Applied Cognitive Psychology* 27 (2013) 150–55.

Rios, Kimberley, et al. "Negative Stereotypes Cause Christians to Underperform in and Disidentify with Science." *Social Psychological and Personality Science* 6 (2015) 959–67.

Rühli, Frank, et al. "Evolutionary Medicine: The Ongoing Evolution of Human Physiology and Metabolism." *Physiology* 31 (2016) 392–97.

Russell, Bertrand. "Is There a God?" (1952).

Sageman, Marc. *Leaderless Jihad: Terror Networks in the Twenty-First Century.* Philadelphia: University of Pennsylvania Press, 2011.

Sandora, McCullen. "The Fine Structure Constant and Habitable Planets. *Journal of Cosmology and Astroparticle Physics* 2016 (2016) 048.

Saniotis, Arthur and Maciej Henneberg. "Anatomical Variations and Evolution: Re-evaluating Their Importance for Surgeons." *ANZ Journal of Surgery* 91 (2021) 837–40.

Schjoedt, Uffe, et al. "Cognitive Resource Depletion in Religious Interactions." *Religion, Brain & Behavior* 3 (2013) 39–55.

———. "The Power of Charisma—Perceived Charisma Inhibits the Frontal Executive Network of Believers in Intercessory Prayer." *Social Cognitive and Affective Neuroscience* 6 (2011) 119–27.

Shariff, Azim F., et al. "Morality and the Religious Mind: Why Theists and Nontheists Differ." *Trends in Cognitive Sciences* 18 (2014) 439–41.

Shen, Fuyuan, et al. "Impact of Narratives on Persuasion in Health Communication: A Meta-analysis." *Journal of Advertising* 44 (2015) 105–13.

Shenhav, Amitai, et al. "Divine Intuition: Cognitive Style Influences Belief in God." *Journal of Experimental Psychology: General* 141 (2012) 423–28.

Sikdar, Debdeep, et al. "Chaos Analysis of Speech Imagery of IPA Vowels." In *International Conference on Intelligent Human Computer Interaction*, 101–10. December 2018.

Smith, James K. A. *Imagining the Kingdom (Cultural Liturgies): How Worship Works.* Grand Rapids: Baker, 2013.

Sosis, Richard, and Eric R. Bressler. "Cooperation and Commune Longevity: A Test of the Costly Signaling Theory of Religion." *Cross-Cultural Research* 37 (2003) 211–39.

Stark, Rodney. "Atheism, Faith, and the Social Scientific Study of Religion." *Journal of Contemporary Religion* 14 (1999) 41–62.

Sutton, Jennifer E., et al. "Geometry Three Ways: An fMRI Investigation of Geometric Information Processing During Reorientation." *Journal of Experimental Psychology: Learning, Memory, and Cognition* 38 (2012) 1530.

Szekely, Raluca D., et al. "Religiosity Enhances Emotion and Deontological Choice in Moral Dilemmas." *Personality and Individual Differences* 79 (2015) 104–09.

Tolentino, Julio Cesar, and Ricardo Bedirian. "Cardiac Autonomic Modulation Related to Prayer May Contribute to the Reduced Cardiovascular Mortality Associated with Religiosity/Spirituality." *J Integr Cardiol Open Access* 2019 (2019) 1–5.

Torrance, Thomas F. *The Ground and Grammar of Theology.* New York: Bloomsbury, 2005.

Van Cappellen, Patty, et al. "Bodily Feedback: Expansive and Upward Posture Facilitates the Experience of Positive Affect. *Cognition and Emotion* (2022) 1–16.

Van Cappellen, Patty, and Megan E. Edwards. "The Embodiment of Worship: Relations Among Postural, Psychological, and Physiological Aspects of Religious Practice." *Journal for the Cognitive Science of Religion* 6 (2018) 56–79.

Wei, Lewen. "Exploring the Effects of Interactive Narratives in Promoting Health Behaviors." MA thesis, 2017.

Wiebe, Philip H. "Religious Experience, Cognitive Science, and the Future of Religion." In *The Oxford Handbook of Religion and Science*, edited by Zachary Simpson, 503–22. Oxford: Oxford University Press, 2006.

Williams, Rowan. *A Ray of Darkness*. Boston: Cowley, 1995.

Withers, Sanford. "The Story of the First Roentgen Evidence." *Radiology* 17 (1931) 99–103.

Wright, N. T. "Mind, Spirit, Soul and Body: All for One and One for All: Reflections on Paul's Anthropology in his Complex Contexts." Society of Christian Philosophers: Regional meeting, Fordham University, March 2011.

Yonker, Julie E., et al. "Primed Analytic Thought and Religiosity: The Importance of Individual Characteristics." *Psychology of Religion and Spirituality* 8 (2016) 298–308.

Ingram Content Group UK Ltd.
Milton Keynes UK
UKHW022105040523
421216UK00003B/5